"Paige, a dear friend and forever my children's favorite teacher, gently reminds us that the beautiful, abundant and overflowing life we crave begins in the still, intimate moments with our creator Dad."

Mark Stuart
– Lead singer of Grammy award winning Audio Adrenaline and Co-Founder of the Hands and Feet Project

My friend, Paige Holloway writes with humor, humility and wisdom. She pulls from her own, personal experiences as a wife and mother to teach us all how to move beyond the chaos of our daily lives and truly quiet our hearts to hear the voice of God. Her stories - coupled with her mature spiritual insight...culminate here in *The Whisperer*, a fresh perspective on hearing our God's still, small voice in an all too often loud and difficult world. I'm so thankful for Paige's heart and how she displays it with each chapter. Moreover, I'm even more thankful that I took the time to read this heart changing book.

Jody McBrayer
– Worship Pastor; Former Lead Singer Christian Music Artist in Pop Quartet; Avalon ; winner of GMA Dove Awards 1998: New Artist of the Year; 1998: Special Event Album of the Year (for their contribution to God With Us); 1999: Inspirational Song of the Year "Adonai"; 1999: Long Form Music Video "My Utmost For His Highest"; 1999: Pop/Contemporary Song of the Year "Testify to Love"

I just finished this sweet book!!!!! I LOVED it!!! My heart is crying. I want more of Christ. This work by Paige Holloway made me hungry for HIM!! We must get this book out to as many as possible. *The Whisperer* is such a love letter to God. It is such and encouraging word for others. My day was made when I read this book.

Diane Van Zandt
– Former Admissions Director at Second Baptist School, Houston, TX; also the Former Director of Education for the Yellowstone Academy. She currently owns Van Zandt Consulting where she does personnel consulting and executive coaching.

Paige Holloway has been our friend and mentor for years. In a world filled with inauthenticity, Paige is a rare glimpse of genuine Christ-like living on display as a wife, mother, bible study leader, and friend. Her book will touch your heart, and fill you with a greater desire to lean in and listen to the whisper of God's leading in your life.

Matthew West
– A multiple-ASCAP Christian Music Songwriter/ Artist of the Year winner, a four-time GRAMMY® nominee, and was awarded his first American Music Award (2013) and a Billboard Music Award (2014).

Our lives are filled with pulls and tugs that distract us from focusing on the important things that surround us: our spouse, our children, our God. Paige Holloway gently reminds us of the importance of prioritizing our focus and in doing so our lives by seeking and desiring God's plan. She clearly shows how one can begin to shift from the frazzled to the calm by slowing down, seeking peace and listening for the still small voice of God as He directs our steps.

William N. Collins, Jr.
– Director of Operations, Laity Lodge Family Camp

Focused passion is magnetic and inspirational. Paige Holloway lives and speaks with this kind of universal enthusiasm. Her heart seems to be ever full and her mind always bright. As her pastor, it thrills me to see her put her collection of thoughts and experiences on paper. The Whisperer is a gift of love and insight that will encourage and empower you to live fully in the grace of God.

Jamie George
– Author, Love Well
Pastor, Journey Church Franklin, TN

THE WHISPERER

THE WHISPERER

Sh'ma: To Hear and Obey

**BY
PAIGE HOLLOWAY**

LUCIDBOOKS

The Whisperer

© Paige Holloway

Published by Lucid Books in Houston, TX.
www.LucidBooks.net

All rights reserved. No part of this publication may be reproduced, stored in a retrieval system, or transmitted in any form by any means, electronic, mechanical, photocopy, recording, or otherwise, without the prior permission of the publisher, except as provided for by USA copyright law.

ISBN 10: 1632960524
ISBN 13: 978-1-63296-052-8
eISBN 10: 1632960532
eISBN 13: 978-1-63296-053-5

Special Sales: Most Lucid Books titles are available in special quantity discounts. Custom imprinting or excerpting can also be done to fit special needs. Contact Lucid Books at info@lucidbooks.net.

It is when I am still I draw near to God.
It is when I am still I can hear.
It is when I am still I can hear my Good Shepherd call me by name.

— Paige Holloway

EPIGRAPH

Then He said, "Go out, and stand on the mountain before the LORD." And behold, the LORD passed by, and a great and strong wind tore into the mountains and broke the rocks in pieces before the LORD, but the LORD was not in the wind; and after the wind an earthquake, but the LORD was not in the earthquake; and after the earthquake a fire, but the LORD was not in the fire; and after the fire a still small voice.

I Kings 19:11-12

DEDICATION

I dedicate my book to my husband Don, who through these almost forty-six years I have known him has shown me true love; a love faithful and unfailing. He has been the example of how, when searching for truth in your story and struggles, to remain hopeful that there is always an answer from God. He has been my beacon and led our family by hearing from God, trusting His Word, believing, and faithfully acting on what he knows to be true.

I also dedicate this book to my children; Barbara, Tillman, Matthew, Sarah, and Rachel who are also the lights of my life. You each have given me the privilege of being your mother as I have the honor to see you grow into the beautiful people and faithful followers of Christ that you are. What a rich life you have given me.

I want to thank my friends who encourage and inspire me daily, and my Editor, Carol Jones, for her diligent work.

CONTENTS

Preface 1

Introduction 7

Prologue: Choosing to Hear from God
Foundational Truths In Hearing His Voice 13

Chapter One: Be Still
Learning to Be In His Presence 21

Chapter Two: Silencing the Enemy
Learning to Replace Lies and Doubt With Truth ... 27

Chapter Three: Soul Mates
Learning to Draw Closer to God by Drawing Closer to Our Spouse 43

Chapter Four: Believe Only
Learning to Believe He Speaks To Us and For Us ... 53

Chapter Five: Deep Calls to Deep
Learning to Follow God's Voice Wherever He Leads ... 63

Chapter Six: Open Doors
Learning to Hear God's Voice in Unforeseen Places ... 77

Chapter Seven: Listen Behind
Learning to Hear and See as God Does 89

Conclusion 103

Epilogue 115

PREFACE

Being a sixty-year old wife of thirty-nine years, mom to five grown and amazing kids, and grandmother to fifteen (so far), qualifies me for nothing short of pure insanity, especially when deciding to take the grand leap of faith to write this book. Except that several people (and especially my son) have encouraged me to do so, I might never have put pen to paper, figuratively, but realistically, finger to keyboard. The consideration of a book written about the wonders of hearing the whispers from God is especially poignant had you known me during the years spent finding my way through the clamor and messes of my family of origin; my mom and dad. Or later in my life, when on any given day you might have seen the laundry piled high on the floor in front of the washer and dryer, the clean indistinguishable from the dirty. I had to stand on the mountain of clothes just to load a new armful into the washer.

You might not have been so eager to pick up a book on the "Whispers of God" authored by me, had you seen me in my early days losing my temper with my ever-so-patient brood, or as I made a scene that might have included angry words thrown around. I frequently used the phrases along the lines of telling children to "Stay in bed!" or "I'll get to you in a minute!" all while a baby was hooked in what seemed to be the permanent nursing position.

Although most in my family might make a good argument for that insanity plea, I have not yet lost all faculties … well, except for a "post-change" body image, some short-term memory loss, and brown hair replaced by gray, only to be colored by Clairol to go back to gray again. I have lost some of my hearing, the use of some fingers with arthritis, and all the confidence my child-rearing days were not riddled with the mistakes I was trying so hard to avoid and now get to mull through in these, my quiet years.

As I attempt to wade through the journey of parts of my life by writing this book, I do hope and pray that what may end up sounding like preachy advice (forgive me ahead of time), is tempered by realizing that the only knowledge I know to be true and unbending is the knowledge of God through Jesus Christ. This is a knowledge that is not from me ... not withholding credit given to all the beautiful teachers I have had in my life, but rests squarely on the shoulders of what I know of God's Word. I pray to be true to Him in what I say, what I write, and that the experiences that have shaped me only give glory to God and His redemptive work.

Having said that, there is plenty I have done that brings little, if any, glory to God. Some has not been much good for anyone or anything other than my own personal tutoring in the time-tested Truth that "all things work together for good to those who love God; to those who are called according to His purpose." Romans 8:28

You see, in those places where I have stumbled and fallen, He has promised to use even those. When I fall so short, it leaves little room for me to slip into self-judging, or self-flagellation, or self-degradation. Rather in my failures, I must remain in Him, knowing He is using weakness to prove strength. In my failures, I must learn to quiet the harsh tone in my head that says, "I'll never be enough." I must render death to those critical voices that say, "I am a failure; I am not lovable ... something's wrong with me!" And with that death comes the pain of dying to self and living as Christ lives in me. It's in dying to myself I can learn then to immerse myself in the gratitude of all that was accomplished on the cross. The knowledge of His love-gift must daily be the cross I carry, the weapon used on the battlefield of my thought-life ... wielded against all the performance-based approval notions, all the hurt and pain that resurfaces, the insecurities, self-judgment, and victim mentality. I must agree with the accuser only to realize and bow knee to the power of God to overcome - not my power to overcome, but His. There is then death to the idea of doing life in my own strength, and lastly, recognition that apart from Him, I can do nothing.

This is a quiet place to inhabit.

> *"Create in me a new heart and renew a right spirit within me, Oh Lord..."* Psalm 51:10

The definition of "create" is insightful when translated from the original Hebrew. It carries a word-picture to help us better understand what God is saying through the Psalmist.

cre·ate
krēˈāt/
in Hebrew: bara
verb
1. Cut Down
2. To Feed As a Formative Process
3. To Make Fat
4. Dispatch[1]

So when King David pleaded with God to "create" in him a clean heart, I wonder if he knew about the heartstring cutting and open surgery, the personal formation and the failing, or that he might then experience the 'dispatch' from God sending him into a "right spirit" (that means 'righteous' - in right-standing) and new life with God. I wonder if David knew it would take more yielding than wielding to possess that "right spirit." I wonder if I also knew

---

1 Strong, James, and James Strong. *The New Strong's Exhaustive Concordance of the Bible: With Main Concordance, Appendix to the Main Concordance, Key Verse Comparison Chart, Dictionary of the Hebrew Bible, Dictionary of the Greek Testament.* Nashville: Thomas Nelson Publishers, 1984.

the cleansing work would include this continual scrubbing out of my wounded and deceitful heart, that I might then live that "full", dispatched and fat, abundant life, without the festering wounds binding me to the old. OUCH! I had no idea!

It is there in that realization, He said to me, "My grace is sufficient for you, for My strength is made complete in weakness. Therefore, most gladly I will rather boast in my infirmities, that the power of Christ may rest upon me; in my weaknesses, His strength is made complete. Therefore, I take pleasure in infirmities, in reproaches, in needs, in persecutions, in distresses, for Christ's sake. For when I am weak, then I am strong." 2 Corinthians 12:9-10

Quite humbling!

Although taking these thoughts captive to the cross is far less glamorous and satisfying for the feeding of my piranha-flesh, and it is counter-intuitive to self-preservation or protection, I learn (usually the hard way) that reliance on Him brings new thoughts and a prevailing quiet in death to my self-sufficient flesh.

I have found this to be the starting place of my work in any relationship. I know the heart issues that stay unresolved in me will only surface when challenged by the patience and endurance required to work in close relationships with others. Oh how the issues point directly to our own heart issues when we really think they are about the other person we are trying so hard to manage. Managing another person is what the world calls codependency and what God calls being discontent to allow the Holy Spirit to refine and transform us. People can draw out of me the worst issues of impatience, short temperedness, hurriedness, and frustration. But just because people draw them out of me doesn't change the fact that they are still "my issues."

I have concluded there is a "whisper" that calls me to find out why, what, who, where, and how. Why is she so difficult to understand? Why am I so misunderstood? Why doesn't he just do what I want? Get what I say? Is it me.... did she not hear me?

PREFACE

Why am I hurting so? Do I have to deal with that heart-issue again? Does he not remember what I said the first time, let alone the three-hundredth time? Where is God in all of this? Why can't I hear Him? Why do I continue to hurt others while they hurt me too?"

Maybe we are missing each other, missing God because we are not hearing each other. Could it be that some answers are only found in a whisper to our hearts and we are rarely still enough to hear? Could it be that we can listen to what lies behind the spoken and hear the unspoken?

We all so often speak in one way but mean something totally different. When someone asks, "How are you?" We answer, "Oh, I'm fine," - when we are not fine. We tend to hide our hurt and pain when in the background we are crying out for ease from our own disappointments and pain. Many times behind the veil of hurt and anger lies an unspoken message that cries for someone to hear. We're much like children in that way. They cry out, "Please, can you see? Please, can you take time to listen? Can you slow down? Please, can you just take the time to listen behind what I am saying and hear the whispers of my heart?"

Slowing our pace helps us hear God as well, helps us listen to what lies behind the thinnest of veils. Behind that veil lies the kingdom whispers, the kingdom of God. In stillness lies the sense that the kingdom of Heaven is near, and the pulse within that kingdom is accessible to our listening hearts. The children in my life were used by God to teach me the whispers and rhythms of God, the whispers of the wounded, and the whispers of a new life born in the kingdom that is within.

He whispers:

"Be still and know that I Am God."
"Be still and know that I Am."
"Be still and know."
"BE STILL."

There are whispers in the silent crevices of my heart ... whispers of love, purpose, direction, correction, and peace. Prayer that holds the whispers of God is not as much words spoken as words heard; a realignment of my soul.

> *"For I have given **to them** the words which You have given Me; and they have received **them**, and have known surely **that** I came forth from You; and they have **believed that** You sent Me."*
> **John 17:8**

I want to look at how God has been speaking to His people throughout the ages and give testimony to how he has spoken to me.

He was speaking then. He is speaking now.

INTRODUCTION

"How do you hear from God?" It is a question that begs an answer, a question I often hear wherever I teach or have the privilege to share my story. It's a question to which some might not even be sure there is an answer. But for me, I am certain there is an answer, and my certainty comes from the extraordinary manner in which God has allowed me to enter His story.

He has directed my journey, watched my steps, and led me into and out of the storms of turbulent waters in my life. He has shown me unfathomable love as I have partaken in this life, endeavoring to hear His voice. God has been there, speaking to my heart, teaching His ways through His Word, and leading me where only he could.

He is the Whisperer to my soul.

So when I am asked, "How do you hear from God?" I understand the depths from which a person asks that question. It's not a question I take lightly, nor an answer I give flippantly. Let me explain.

Hearing HIS Voice

I was once told "hearing from God" was sacrilegious. The woman who told me this said, "Who do you think you are anyway ... that you would hear from God Himself?" (Almost as if I was entirely foolish in my attempt to hear from a distant-on-the-throne-high-in-the-sky-God.)

I am no great matriarch recorded in the halls of faith, nor am I a renowned Bible scholar that draws attendance from great crowds of people who are searching for the truth. So who am I that I can hear from God? I am not unlike the characters I read about in the Bible, a flawed soul, interested in following Christ, hearing from God, and being led by the Holy Spirit.

I have learned that as a woman who desires to hear from the Lord, there are many voices I must learn to differentiate from His. First, there are the old tapes in my head from my mother and father, and then the tapes that come from unhealthy roles I have played throughout life. Additionally, there are the voices of the people in my life who love me and want what is best for me. And lastly, there is the voice of my own gut, desiring to be wanted and loved. In learning to differentiate between those many voices, I think I have discovered certain keys to unlock some mysteries about hearing from God.

Jesus speaks of Himself as our Shepherd. He warns us not to listen to the voice of the false shepherds but to instead hear His voice and follow Him. He says He will lead us, protect us, and if we do not hear His voice, we must not be one of His sheep. I take that to mean it is in my heart's deepest desire to "hear from God" - to belong to Him so that His voice is clear and to hear Him so I can figure out how to make sense of this life. I want to know Him and be known; just as the sheep who knows and follows his shepherd; just as the sheep that heeds his shepherd's voice and obeys his commands.

I have believed God's voice enough in obedience to risk important things and relationships in my journey. It can be challenging, even frightening, to hear a command from God, as it most always demands a response.

Jesus, my Shepherd, says the way I love Him is to obey His Word. In order to obey His Word, I must first listen; I must hear. So, I have to ask these questions relative to that command:

Who am I listening to?
What am I hearing, and what response does it require?
Where is His voice coming from?
What does it sound like to hear from God?

How can I know that it is Him?
Why must I listen?

I have to admit, I am afraid of the answers to some of these questions, as they all require an active response from me. It is in that response that I show my love for Him, my Shepherd.

In my attempt to write the answers to these questions, I remember the miraculous ways God has spoken to me. My story is filled with the details of a love narrated by a woman who sometimes finds herself observing from the sidelines all that God is doing. I have found that many times the listening and hearing have required me to step out in a faith that knows no journey's end and asks of me more than I think I can give. It is in these stories that I attempt to build memorial stones; an altar of worship that glorifies the Author of all I am. It is in the tiny details of the narratives that I can see Him leading, speaking to me, and showing me His heart.

The Stories are the Lessons

I was once told the best way to write about hearing from God was to drive heavy on the Bible lessons themselves and use the "stories" almost as you would flannel-graphs or teaching aids in Sunday school, as examples to support biblical truth. But to me, inherent in the stories is the very life of Christ Himself. It is there that He guides me, and as I listen, He unquestionably is leading me toward one end, to know HIS LOVE. Every journey, every story, leads to His LOVE.

Who am I listening to and what am I hearing? I must learn to discern the voices that fill my thought life every day.

- Does that voice contradict the Word of God?
- Does it tell me I am not who God says I am?
- Is the thought or message able to be reconciled to God's Word?

- Is it the world's influence or is it influence from the relationships I have cultivated?
- Is it true? If not, what am I doing to discard my belief in a lie?
- What response must I give to the whispers I hear?
- Where is His voice coming from?
- What does it sound like and how can I be sure it is Him?

I believe we can hear God's voice in many ways. I often press pause in my everyday life and observe the messages God sends to me. I may see the glimmer in my grandson's eyes. I may hear the wind just outside my window and feel the breeze brush my face and remember how blessed I am. I may smell the pine or orange essence as I prepare my home or meals and it conjures in me gratefulness in the moment. I may hear a lecture or sermon that stirs the Holy Spirit in me to draw closer to His presence. I may read in His word, the Bible, and hear His voice calling me to deeper relationship with Him. I may hear a friend speak truth into my heart and change the way I react to the new things God is making in me. I may hear a direct whisper in my ear; a pause of truth shared directly from God Himself; through His Holy Spirit that beckons me to turn this way or that. I may ponder it long in my heart. It may resonate deep in my soul a connection with my Creator, Father, Friend, Comforter, and Savior, so much that my only response can be obedience and praise.

Why must I listen? Because God says this:

> "He also taught me, and said to me: "Let your heart retain my words; Keep my commands, and live." Proverbs 4:4

> "My son, keep my words, And treasure my commands within you." Proverbs 7:1

INTRODUCTION

> *"Jesus answered and said to him, "If anyone loves Me, he will keep My word; and My Father will love him, and We will come to him and make Our home with him."* John 14:23

Timothy Keller writes in his book, *Jesus the King*, of Mark the gospel author. He writes of Mark the storyteller who narrates Jesus' life in the details. Mark's firsthand accounts of all he experiences of Jesus continue to speak volumes to his audience. Those detailed accounts of Jesus interfacing in the ordinary lives of people are the testimonies of Christ Himself. Every word of those accounts is pregnant with meaning, with the presence of God Himself. It was the breath of heaven speaking through ordinary men in an extraordinary theater and timeline of their lives. Their obedience to heed the "call" of their Savior makes me pause to think His same voice that was available then is available now and forever… "to them that believe." So…I believe. And I try to account in the ordinary, but extraordinary, theater of my life and timeline, the testimonies of God's sweet whispers. He says He dances over me with singing.

I can hear Him.

PROLOGUE:
CHOOSING TO HEAR FROM GOD
Foundational Truths In Hearing His Voice

It seems somehow contrarian to title a chapter "Choosing to Hear from God" as though a believer might choose otherwise. But hearing from God requires a conscious effort on our part. It is a decision to spend time in His presence, reading his Word, shutting out other voices we are accustomed to hearing, listening for His voice, and then responding and acting. The entire process of hearing from God requires us to choose not only to hear, but also to respond and obey.

In her book, *Walking in the Dust of Rabbi Jesus,* author Lois Tverberg explains that while it might seem that hearing and then obeying is a two-step process, in reality it is one action. Here's what she wrote:

"The Hebrew words that Jesus quoted from Deuteronomy overflow with great wisdom. Looking more closely, this is how the first line of the Sh'ma is translated: Sh'ma (Hear) Israel, Adonai (the Lord) elohenu (our God) Adonai (the Lord) echad! (one/alone). The first word, Sh'ma, we usually translate "hear." But the word Sh'ma has a much wider, deeper meaning than "to perceive sound." It encompasses a whole spectrum of ideas that includes listening, taking heed, and responding with action to what one has heard.

For instance, in English we read Deuteronomy 11:13 as, "So if you faithfully obey the commands I am giving you today…" Literally, though, this verse reads, "And it will be if hearing, you will hear…" And after Moses recited the covenant to the people of Israel, they responded, "We will do everything the LORD has said; we will obey" (Exodus 24:7). But the Hebrew here actually reads, "All that God has said we will do and we will hear." The two verbs here are really synonymous - to hear is to do, to be obedient."[2]

In I Samuel 3:1-10, we see Samuel, a young prophet, hearing a voice as he lay down to sleep, an occurrence that happened three nights in a row. Each night that Samuel heard the voice, he got up and went to Eli, the Chief Priest, and said, "You called me?" to which Eli replied, "It wasn't I, go back to bed." But on the third night, Eli realized Samuel was hearing the voice of God and instructed him to go back to bed, and when he heard God's voice again to respond, "Yes, Lord. Your servant hears you." Samuel did exactly as Eli commanded. He waited to hear God's voice and when he heard it, he responded.

God spoke a prophecy to Samuel that night, one that changed the face of Israel.

But why couldn't Samuel recognize it was the Lord speaking to him? Well first of all, it wasn't his role in the temple. Typically, the Lord spoke only to the Chief Priest, so Samuel wasn't accustomed to the sound of God's voice. And secondly, he did not have the completed Scriptures of God to read and meditate.

Today, we as followers of Jesus Christ can hear the voice of God and have the benefit of the completed scriptures to guide us in discerning what He wants us to do. But even with such incredible blessing, as children of God, we must decide two things: that hearing from God is vital and is as important as life itself, and that acting upon what we hear is just as critical. We must choose both to hear and obey His voice.

How Do We Choose?

How do we choose to hear and obey His voice? We must learn to set aside our busy and demanding lives and practice being in

---

[2] Tverberg, Lois. *Walking in the Dust of Rabbi Jesus: How the Jewish Words of Jesus Can Change Your Life.* Grand Rapids, Mich.: Zondervan, 2011.

His presence. In doing so, we become hungry to hear from Him. A beautiful way to whet our appetite for Him is to immerse ourselves in Him.

- Use Christian music, broadcasts, workshops, or blogs to keep Him ever-present in the space of the mind.
- Listen to sermons, counselors, teaching, and Christian friends when renewing the mind to agree with God and His Word.
- Ask for a continuous cleansing of the heart and for God to place protection around a heart that can easily slip into the ways that draw us away from God. **James 4:8 says,** "Draw near to God, and He will draw near to you. Cleanse your hands, you who have sinned; and purify your hearts, you who are double minded."

The more time we spend with God, the more we will hear His voice. And the more we hear his voice (and obey what we hear), the more we will continue to hear from Him.

It is not enough to simply hear from God, though. Hearing requires action. In Luke, 6:46-49, God tells us that hearing and obeying are inextricable and that doing so builds the foundation of our lives on solid ground. This is how we dance together in the rhythms of the kingdom of God.

> *"And why call ye me, Lord, Lord, and do not the things, which I say? Whosoever comes to me, and hears my sayings, and does them, I will show you to whom he is like:He is like a man who built a house, and dug deep, and laid the foundation on a rock; and when the flood arose, the stream beat vehemently upon that house, and could not shake it for it was founded upon a rock. But he that hears, and does not, is like a man that without a*

foundation built a house upon the earth, against which the stream did beat vehemently, and immediately it fell; and the ruin of that house was great." Luke 6:46-49

God is speaking to us in these passages. He is clear about the importance of "hearing," teaching us that we possess "hearing ears," spiritual ears, given to us by God, the ears of our hearts open to the promptings of the Holy Spirit. He admonishes that upon hearing and obeying, we are given the measure that we then have to give. He promises that as we trust Him in obedience, we are given more, just as He said in Mark 4:24, *"And he said unto them, Take heed what you hear: with what measure you are given, it shall be measured to you: and unto you that hear shall more be given."* The prompting is described by God as a still, small voice. He is not heard in the wind, earthquakes and not the fire…. but in the small, still voice.

1 Kings 19:11-12 says, *"And he said, Go forth, and stand upon the mount before the Lord. And, behold, the Lord passed by, and a great and strong wind rent the mountains, and break in pieces the rocks before the Lord; but the Lord was not in the wind; and after the wind an earthquake; but the Lord was not in the earthquake. And after the earthquake a fire; but the Lord was not in the fire: and after the fire a still small voice."*

As I said, it is a choice. If we are too busy to spend time with God, cultivating our relationship with Him, learning from His word, and desiring our hearts to be cleansed, His still small voice will be silenced by the sheer volume of everything else in our lives.

Why Is Hearing From God So Difficult?

I am often asked why hearing from God is so difficult, or I hear statements that question the reality of hearing God's voice at all. When this happens, my first thought goes back to what He asks: "Why do you not do what I asked of you, and yet you call yourself mine?" When was the last time hearing from God did not immediately and innately include obedience to His voice? I think too often we do not realize that hearing from God requires a quick response in our hearts, a posture of humble obedience. After all, God is mostly interested in our heart attitude. If we think we are not hearing from God, we must go back to the last time we think we heard Him and check to see if obedience quickly followed. If not, then obey the call and heed the word. It is only then that our "house," our spiritual connection to God, and our spiritual ears have their foundation built upon the rock of God. It is a sure foundation, one that holds us in times of need, keeps us in our sorrow, and leads us in His ways. It is in the practicing of the presence of God that our ears are trained and our hearing made more acute. It is not enough just to fine-tune the hearing; to obey is the response He requires.

> *"For if any be a hearer of the word, and not a doer, he is like unto a man beholding his natural face in a glass: For he beholds himself, and goes his way, and straightway forgets what manner of man he was. But whoso looks into the perfect law of liberty, and continues therein, he being not a forgetful hearer, but a doer of the work, this man shall be blessed in his deed."* James 1:23-25

How Do We Know It Is From God?

Jesus tells us in John 10:4 that "... *the sheep follow him because they know his voice."* Confirmation of God's word to us can be difficult to discern. How can we know it is God and not Satan or some outside influence, family conditioning, or our natural bent toward selfishness? Ask the Holy Spirit to reveal Scripture to validate the voice of God. After all, God will never contradict His Word and He can never lie. Satan will use scripture to try to deceive us and make us afraid. A "fear" response is not from God. If we are reacting in fear, then we know the voice must be counterfeit. The good news is we can use scripture to counteract fear:

2 Timothy 1:7 says, *"For God hath not given us the spirit of fear; but of power, and of love, and of a sound mind."* When we understand that, we then realize God's word will create peace in us, and He will never lie or contradict Himself. It is important to cast down thoughts contrary to His Word and bring them into agreement with God Himself. There are several competing voices that do have spiritual significance and we must distinguish those as we endeavor to hear from God. We hear from God the Father, the Son, and the Holy Spirit, His angels including Satan and demonic forces, and our own soul's resound. The soul is the space of our mind, will, and emotions. We can trust these only when we are born again of spirit and when we have submitted their control to that of the Holy Spirit. Renewing of the mind becomes vital as we learn the ways of the Spirit, and we walk according to the Spirit and not the voices of our un-renewed mind, will, or emotion. It is beautiful when we can distinguish and discern the whispers of God and wade through all of the voices that compete for His time with us. Settling on the fact that He loves us and wants what's best for us increases our faith and prompts us to trust Him in all we hear. He does not deceive.

> *"For though we walk in the flesh, we do not war after the flesh: (For the weapons of our warfare are not carnal, but mighty through God to the pulling down of strong holds;) Casting down imaginations, and every high thing that exalts itself against the knowledge of God, and bringing into captivity every thought to the obedience of*

Christ; And having in a readiness to revenge all disobedience, when your obedience is fulfilled."
II Corinthians 10:3-6

"That by two immutable things, in which it was impossible for God to lie, we might have a strong consolation, who have fled for refuge to lay hold upon the hope set before us." Hebrews 6:18

    This truth is unchangeable: God cannot coexist with lies. Since His name is Truth, it is contrary to His very existence for Him to lie. Therefore, He is trustworthy when we are able to discern and hear His voice.

    When we desire to hear the voice of God, when we choose to practice His presence in our lives, our faith and trust in Him grows and our purpose in this life becomes evident.

CHAPTER ONE:
BE STILL
Learning to Be In His Presence

"Carry some quiet around inside thee," the well-known Quaker, George Fox, used to say. "Be still and cool in thy own mind and spirit, from thy own thoughts, and then thou wilt feel the principle of God to turn thy mind to the Lord from whence cometh life; whereby thou may receive the strength and power to allay all storms and tempests."[3]

I used to make a routine that included tucking my five children into bed at night. Every evening, without fail, I made the rounds of "Good-nights," and "I need a drink of water," and "Shut the door but only a crack - oh wait that's too much! Oh that's just right." After all seemed settled, when I was sure "not a creature was stirring, not even a mouse," I slipped back into their rooms and knelt beside each of their five beds and asked God to lead me in hearing Him on behalf of their small, but very significant lives. I listened more than I talked to God, and invariably He spoke to me subtly about the specific needs for

---

[3] Thurman, Howard. "The Inward Sea." In *Meditations of the Heart*, 22. New York: Harper, 1953.

each child. It was a quiet place where I heard His whisper, and it was in solitude where I received revelation about what needs lay in my children's hearts.

My ministry to my family started there on my knees. I have walked all these many years humbled and forced to my knees. Humbled, because raising five children is taxing. It carries a weight of helplessness, presses you right to the edge, and then pulls you back. It comes with moments of exhaustion and extreme exhilaration, defeat, and default. It was there on my knees that I was able to hear the heartfelt needs of a son mistreated and rejected by best friends, and found crying in the night because of deep wounds of rejection and cruelty. It was there I prayed for my daughter and her budding, preteen friendships and where I heard God leading me. It was there I prayed for my children's future spouses and asked for guidance and wisdom for them. It was in that listening posture I found help when my children and I needed direction. It was there I asked God for wisdom concerning how to balance our five children's needs and for an infusion of energy as I tried to be present and attentive with each one.

I believe that this was the place of "stillness" not only for revelation, but also comfort for me and something that I carried over into my relationship with my husband, Don. Dependence on God became a way of life, of worship, of stillness in the midst of storms. Christ gave first, I offered back to Him, and He gave again. The rhythm of the kingdom was experienced there.

Prayer is often the quiet place where the heart can be still. It is where the whisper of our Father can soothe our aching thoughts and teach us what to do in times where we have few answers to life's heartache. I learned to practice this presence and quietness. It didn't come naturally, but as I learned to be still, I learned to recognize the sound of His voice. It is in His presence, alone and still, that I can hear God's whispers, and it is there that I align my heart and mind with the will and Word of God.

It Starts With Me

There is an old shed at the back of my property. It's covered with vines and spider webs, is dug out and under by moles, and filled with antique farm tools. There is fractured light inside, and the minimal life once found there was over time choked out by the overgrown mess that now covers the entrance and windows of this little shed. My heart is like that house when I fail to subject it to the work of God. No entrance, no light, no place to inhabit. My heart is covered with the vines of the cares of this world and the deceptions this life brings.

Jeremiah 17:9 tells us, *"The heart is deceitful above all things, and desperately wicked; Who can know it?"*

... BUT GOD.

When I forget to acknowledge His presence even in the smallest way, the deficit will carry over into every area of my life. My relationships and how well I function in them are directly related to how much time I spend with my Father in Heaven. There is a direct proportionality to how much of my heart, mind, thought-life, and time I yield to the control of the Holy Spirit and the teachings of Christ, and how well I can love and function in my relationships. It is still, even then, only my yielding to Him and the life of Christ in me that I can have the connectedness I need to function in a healthy life with others.

My Training Ground

My training ground for hearing from God has been best experienced through the life of my ever-patient and precious family. My relationship with them is the greatest evidence of the time I spend with Him, hearing from Him and obeying what He teaches me. When I am able to live in self-denial, yielding to the leading of the Holy Spirit, I have experienced fruit in those relationships. When I am controlling out of fear and lack of trust; I have choked the life out of the ones I love.

My ability to hear the Lord and have a God-pleasing relationship with my family has come from being:

First, a follower of Jesus, submitting my life and my eternity to the saving grace of his redemptive death on the cross.

Second, a wife to the love of my life from my youth, always believing my heart and mind are one with my spouse even if I cannot always feel it so. In learning self-denial, I open trust and intimacy in my relationship with my husband. I trust God's work in him without thinking it's my job to rule and control. I take care of myself by asking for God's help in loving my husband with the love that can only come from yielding to the Holy Spirit's reign in my heart. I receive love and ask for what I may need from him. I am committed to life with him, through struggles and hurts, joy and sorrows. I know full well the love of God is expressed through my husband's ability to lay his life down for me and through his unwavering love for and submission to God.

Lastly, a mother raising, training, teaching, and loving my five children. Not exactly a degreed or even prestigious program for learning, but it is where I learned. My precious ones have taught me so much about the whispers of God as I have had to rely heavily on seeing not with my natural eyes but with spiritual eyes. Children often give us unspoken signals of stress and pain. As I learned to "listen behind" what they might be saying and respond to their needs, my ears were finely tuned to the needs of their hearts. I practiced listening to their hearts even when their mouths were saying otherwise, and I tried to hear what God would have me resonate back to them. Resonating is a way that hearts can touch. One expresses needs, and like a sound box vibrating, the absorption and understanding of that need is resounded back with love, touch, and gentle validation. I have watched how children's hearts can be opened in this way and how the whispers of their hearts are instruments to teach hearing the whispers of God. It becomes a heart-to-heart connection where love can be shared and trust is cultivated.

Let the Children Come

Just as my family was my training ground for hearing the whispers of God, I know that I am also their training ground. Children learn about life from the experiences they have interacting with those around them. As adults, it is our job to teach them how to love, trust, and communicate with others. How well we do this greatly affects the relationship they will someday have with God.

Unfortunately, because of language barriers, immaturity, false cues, and our own busy lives, adults often struggle to carefully and thoughtfully interact with children. Our responses to them, more often than not, may feel hurried, bothered, or just generally disinterested. Children can seem almost alien, like foreigners speaking some strange and indistinguishable language.

This leads to children often being misunderstood and overlooked, dishonored and disrespected. Take for example the numbers of times we have all been out somewhere, in a store or maybe a restaurant. A child cries, then screams, and the parents or caregivers just keep saying things that make the pain escalate until eventually the child yells and falls to the floor, as if he or she has just been assaulted. We say things like, "Just stop your crying." We whisper under our breath to avoid our own shame, "You are being such a baby! What's the matter with you?" or "You are so frustrating!" I've seen children jerked by the arm, pulled and dragged, slapped and hit, pinched and squeezed. I've heard children's requests go unheard until the tenth or fifteenth time they ask. Then suddenly, when the adult finally realizes the child is talking, they are promptly told to be quiet. I've seen (and done it myself) adults who answer the questions of the persistent child with an obligatory answer by just saying, "Mmm hmmm," or "Uh huh," all while tuning out the child completely and never truly hearing the request. The message we communicate when we do this is that whatever we are obsessed with in our minds takes higher precedence than hearing the needs of our children.

I know a child must learn to wait, to be patient, and learn important social skills like not interrupting, but I am referring to the day-to-day ignoring of the voice of the little ones.

When we consistently interact with our children in such ways, we send a subliminal message that says they are not important. Instead, we might try getting on our knees in front of a child's eyes, slowing down our speech, quieting our agendas and ourselves, and stopping to actually hear them. Additionally, we might ask God to give us particular insights into their little hearts. Taking that same time and listening well to the heart of a child might create a special moment of understanding. A whispering in the heart of both, once again creating that heart connection that is so important.

Because we know the way we respond to our children's needs affects how they will respond to God, we must not allow our busy, rushed lives to prevent our children from hearing the whispers of the Kingdom. Jesus said it this way, *"Prevent not the little children to come unto Me, for theirs is the kingdom of heaven." Matthew 19:14*

As we give our busy lives over to God and learn to live in His presence, our hearts are more readily connected to the heart of God. When we take the time in our lives to be still and allow these heart moments, it leads us to love others well. Loving well is experiencing the kingdom of God. The whispers of His kingdom are all around. We have only to be still and learn to listen for the sound of His voice.

CHAPTER TWO:
SILENCING THE ENEMY
Learning to Replace Lies and Doubt With Truth

It is God who whispers to me on a daily basis and is faithful to complete that work which He has begun in me. But before hearing the whispers of God in His Kingdom and the call to hearing these whispers in relationships, the other whispers in the rhythms of this world must be continually quieted and settled.

Make no mistake about it; there is an enemy who tries to whisper to me, distracting me from the voice of God. This enemy wants me to hear:

> I am not qualified.
> I am not loved.
> I will never measure up.
> I must always defend and justify myself.

But it is God, who by and through His Word and in His presence counters the accusations of the enemy of my soul. He says to me:

> "You are precious. "
> "You are mine."

"You are loved."
"You are beautiful in my sight."

So why is it so difficult to silence the voice of the enemy? Because Satan is cunning, and crafty, and will stop at nothing to get us to believe his lies. Notice his accusations are always in the first person? Satan is very persistent in the way he speaks his lies over me, making them easier for me to believe. He uses lies that sound like truth, lies that tell me I will never outlive my past sins, and lies that this world would have me believe. He leads me to doubt myself and God's power within me, and tells me that I will forever be unloved.

Lies That Sound Like Truth

The "I am not qualified" message from Satan that slips into my closet of confidence must be dealt with in the framework of God's Word. The thing about Satan is he takes what is true, and then he distorts it into something that is categorically not true.

Remember when Satan used God's Word to torment Jesus in the desert? Satan recognized that Jesus was weakened from hunger after being in the desert for 40 days. He seized the opportunity to torment Jesus. He said to Him, "***IF*** you are the Son of God, throw yourself down. Surely God will rescue you, for it is written," and then he quotes these verses from the Book of Psalms:

> *"The Lord will command his angels to take good care of you.*
> *They will lift you up in their hands.*
> *Then you won't trip over a stone."* Psalm 91:11-12

It is true that God can and does protect His children. But it is also true that we are to use good judgment and not push the limits with God.

In reply, Jesus fought Satan's twisted truth with pure Truth. He said, *"It is also written, 'Do not put the Lord your God to the test.'"* Deuteronomy 6:16

Following Jesus' example, I take the lies Satan whispers in my mind, and I compare them to what is true. When Satan tells me, "I am not qualified," I speak what is truth to silence his voice.

It is TRUE; I am NOT qualified. I'm not. Not on my own anyway. It is only in facing my adversary and living in the present reality of Jesus' qualifications that I truly know God's credentials are enough. He loves me, and I am His. It is His signet ring of qualification that I bear in an authority over the influence and power of worldly kingdoms. He says I am the righteousness of God in Christ Jesus.

> *"Blessed are those who hunger and thirst for righteousness, for they shall be filled."* Matthew 5:6

> *"But seek first the kingdom of God and His righteousness, and all these things shall be added to you."* Matthew 6:33

Knowledge of this Truth opens the heavenly Kingdom and gives access to a love that renews me and makes me whole.

Condemning Lies from My Past

Satan would have me believe the sins from my victimized and unguided past would render me forever unlovable. This is the cornerstone of Satan's lies – that we are not loved for a myriad of reasons. However, his argument is up against a God who literally embodies love. And so again, I must look at Satan's lies through the context of God's Truth.

I am loved. Or so it says in God's Word. I must settle what I believe. I personally can testify to the boundless love that Jesus had for one who was first so lost, and was then plucked from fear and selfishness into a life of gratefulness. I kneel to the One who holds it all. My life was supposed to look like the statistics of my family tree: the alcoholic, divorced, cheating, lying, suicidal, depressed, manipulative, sexually addicted, heart-broken, desperate person whose path and life-plan were prepared for her by generations of lost and lonely hearts, and reinforced by her life experiences. Our experiences of pain in this life are where we will draw many of our conclusions about God. For example, if our fathers are neglectful and distant, we may conclude God is also like our earthly fathers. In reality, it is what God says in His Word that we believe by faith. It is by using this Word, our only offensive weapon, that we can battle the thoughts that keep us from renewing our minds to agree with the Word of God and what God says is true. He says He is our Father and that *"every good and perfect gift comes from the Father of Lights." (James 1:17)* He says He loves us like an "Abba" or daddy. His character of gentleness, presence, and kindness are lovingly shown us through the person of Jesus Christ. This is where we can substitute what we believe in the lies with the Truth of who God is and what He says. We are then listening to His whispers that bring hope, love, joy, peace, gratitude, and faith.

It is His love for me that bears witness to the truth of Galatians 2:20 which says, *"I have been crucified with Christ; it is no longer I who live, but Christ lives in me; and the life, which I now live in the flesh I live by faith in the Son of God, who loved me and gave Himself for me."*

The Lies of This World

Then there are lies this world wants me to believe. These are the lies that tell me I will never be enough. They tell me that I must work harder and be more to be loved and significant. Believing those lies makes me strive and causes stress and a lack of peace. It can cause me to spin into performance-based acceptance patterns that rob me of joy and rest.

What about the lie I believe regarding comparison? I have to rearrange my thoughts about being measured by some hard and strict (not to mention made-up) measuring stick; one that pounds me down and whispers in my ear that there's no way I could ever be as good as others around me. The constant comparison that goes on in my head about who is good, better, and best rarely includes me. I take the enemy's bait - hook, line and sinker, and I believe "never will I quite make it."

But the voice of God says, "You, my precious dear, are sitting here with Me in a heavenly place. Not bound to this earth and all its trappings and pain; but with Me. I love you. You are mine." Again, He tells us in Ephesians 2:6, "And God raised us up together with Christ, and made us sit together in the heavenly places."

Imagine we are invited to sit near Jesus as He sits at the right hand of the Father. We are one with Him and the Father, as He has desired. In that place, the measuring stick of this world is broken in two. Picture this: Sitting right by Him, the One with all Authority, all Knowledge, all of the Kingdom at His feet. Sitting right there with Him, where His love for us has no measure. It is endless and His desire is to be with us in His unconditional and extravagant love.

It is there, in that place, He whispers, "I love you dearest one, come be with Me. I love you."

I remember this when I believe somehow I'll never be enough. I was not created to be "good enough." I was created to rely on God as enough, just Him and Only Him. He is the only One who gives me that seat; that place right next to Him. It is not what I earned or can ever be "good enough" to deserve. He gives it to me freely. It should produce an attitude of gratefulness but how quickly I slip into the old patterns of thought, becoming downtrodden, triggered in pain, bound and hurt. Remember to express my gratitude? Hurting others back, showing I can control, and leaning into resentments and anger is the tumble of a free-fall back to the old ways. I fall so short and yet, well, I am mysteriously His! I am mystically loved and a treasure to be obtained far greater than pearls of great price. It is a great mystery of faith. It is the dichotomous mystery of unconditional and unearned love.

A Change of Heart is Required

When looking for truth and hearing the whispers of His Kingdom, shutting off the lies that sound like truth, the lies once believed, and the lies of this world, becomes paramount. But at times, experiences in relationships with others can trigger negative responses in us that allow us to believe the lies of the enemy. If we have a fighting chance at silencing the voice of the enemy, we must thoroughly examine our hearts for any unresolved heart conditions. Our negative response to situations is like cords inside our hearts attached to lies we may have believed in our past or that we believe now.

For example,

- A child who was given up at birth might carry around a cord of rejection attached to a lie that says he is unloved.
- A woman who used to be promiscuous might carry around a cord of shame attached to a lie that says she will always be that girl.
- A man who was abused as a child might carry around a cord of rebellion attached to a lie that he must always be in control.

These cords can be strong motivators in the heart, motivators that might lead one to believe the enemy's lies, motivators that tell us we are something different than who God says we are to Him. When tugged, these cords can pull at so many bundled feelings and unsettled ideas, luring our thoughts and reactions toward something different than what God says about our value and worth.

For example, my children (picture me about 30 years old) once demanded from me, all at once, all their different needs. It happened frequently. It was normal and their needs were normal. It seemed that as the day ended and evening rolled in, the intensity of their desire for my attention grew to a raised pitch of demand and fear. Somehow it seemed that their needs called out to be met all at the same time. The negative energy in the house elevated and tears, both theirs and mine, began to flow.

One would be pulling me to help with homework, while at the same time one needed a diaper change; one needed to be taken to music, while one was crying from hunger, and still one was crying because he or she needed a nap. If these needs crashed down all at the same time, while a boiling pot of spaghetti was overflowing on the stove and just after receiving the call that daddy was coming home a little bit late, my response began to draw power from some of my unresolved, childhood memories and lies I had believed for so long.

I didn't know it at the time, but being overwhelmed had its origins in having to raise my little sister in a highly dysfunctional and alcoholic home. I was ill-equipped at the age of five to begin responsibility for my sister; protecting her, feeding her, putting her down for naps, making sure she was clean and taken care of. I was neither equipped nor capable of meeting her demands and need for love. But even now, as I get overwhelmed with demands on my time, the fear of "not being enough" becomes powerfully real. What's not real is the notion that I cannot handle it as an adult. What is real is that there was a time in my life when I definitely was "not enough," nor should I have been put in the position to try to be enough. Now as a more emotionally integrated adult, I actually can change a diaper; turn off the stove, answer homework problems, and take children where they need to go. I can do this without triggers pulling me into a feeling of being overwhelmed. I can do so not because I am more able, but because of a great inner healing and relinquishing of control.

Learning to practice the presence of God's healing power in the midst of feeling overwhelmed is how to press through our troubles and silence the voice of the enemy. When we give each thought, idea, and feeling of powerlessness and insecurity over to God's control, it trains our spiritual ears to hear His peaceful voice in the midst of chaos. He becomes Counselor even when our acknowledgement of the need for one is faint. Years of ongoing therapy from The Counselor allows Jesus an opportunity to shape our hearts and minds, teach us new words and responses, and change our old thoughts and destructive patterns. As our hearts are changed, we can take action in stressful situations without allowing the enemy's voice to convince us of lies we know are simply untrue.

Overcoming Doubt

Sometimes, though, even when we are sure we are hearing from God, it's easy to doubt what He is saying to us. This is another ploy the enemy uses to convince us we cannot hear God's voice. Read how he used this tactic with Moses.

> *"Now Moses was tending the flock of Jethro his father-in-law, the priest of Midian. And he led the flock to the back of the desert, and came to Horeb, the mountain of God. And the Angel of the Lord appeared to him in a flame of fire from the midst of a bush. So he looked, and behold, the bush was burning with fire, but the bush was not consumed. Then Moses said, "I will now turn aside and see this great sight, why the bush does not burn."* Exodus 3:1-3

Notice how Moses was just going about his regular business of the day and was not really expecting to hear from God? Sometimes hearing God's voice requires us to take notice of things around us. Moses was able to sense God's presence by noticing the fire was not consuming the bush. The story continues:

> *"So when the Lord saw that he turned aside to look, God called to him from the midst of the bush and said, "Moses, Moses!" And he said, "Here I am."Then He said, "Do not draw near this place. Take your sandals off your feet, for the place where you stand is holy ground." Moreover He said, "I am the God of your father—the God of Abraham, the God of Isaac, and the God of Jacob." And Moses hid his face, for he was afraid to look upon God."* Exodus 3:4-6

When Moses responded to the call of God, he also obeyed the immediate instructions from God. He was not to approach the presence of God without the reverence due in the holiness of the moment. It truly is a holy moment to hear from God. As God draws near to us, we are near Him. The kingdom of Heaven is near.

> *"And the Lord said: "I have surely seen the oppression of My people who are in Egypt, and have heard their cry because of their taskmasters, for I know their sorrows. So I have come down to deliver them out of the hand of the Egyptians, and to bring them up from that land to a good and large land, to a land flowing with milk and honey, to the place of the Canaanites and the Hittites and the Amorites and the Perizzites*

> *and the Hivites and the Jebusites. Now therefore, behold, the cry of the children of Israel has come to Me, and I have also seen the oppression with which the Egyptians oppress them. Come now, therefore, and I will send you to Pharaoh that you may bring My people, the children of Israel, out of Egypt."* Exodus 3:7-10

God called Moses to lead His people out of bondage into freedom. In this example, God laid down a foreshadowing of Christ. He showed us the picture of Christ present and pre-eminent from the beginning of His story. God showed His compassion and mercy for His people and chose Moses to lead them out of Egypt. In this way, Moses was a "type" of Christ. Notice how God was "sending" and Moses was not going out from under God's protection and instruction? It is important for us to remember our own limitations when we are obeying the Father's voice. We make ourselves totally dependent on the Father's strength to lead us.

> *"But Moses said to God, "Who am I that I should go to Pharaoh, and that I should bring the children of Israel out of Egypt?" So He said, "I will certainly be with you. And this shall be a sign to you that I have sent you: When you have brought the people out of Egypt, you shall serve God on this mountain."* Exodus 3:11-12

Moses' first reaction to being called by God was doubt. Surely God didn't think Moses was the one to lead God's people? It was the self-doubt Moses carried with him that made him question his ability to follow God. But Moses pressed on, because he knew he was in the presence of God.

> "Then Moses said to God, "Indeed, when I come to the children of Israel and say to them, 'The God of your fathers has sent me to you,' and they say to me, 'What is His name?' what shall I say to them?" Exodus 3:13

Moses wanted to establish in whose authority he would bring this word. Perhaps he was chosen by God because of that humility? God answered Moses by telling him the great authority in whom he would be sanctioned.

> "And God said to Moses, "I AM WHO I AM." And He said, "Thus you shall say to the children of Israel, 'I AM has sent me to you.'" Moreover God said to Moses, "Thus you shall say to the children of Israel: 'The Lord God of your fathers, the God of Abraham, the God of Isaac, and the God of Jacob, has sent me to you. This is My name forever, and this is My memorial to all generations.' Go and gather the elders of Israel together, and say to them, 'The Lord God of your fathers, the God of Abraham, of Isaac, and of Jacob, appeared to me, saying, "I have surely visited you and seen what is done to you in Egypt; and I have said I will bring you up out of the affliction of Egypt to the land of the Canaanites and the Hittites and the Amorites and the Perizzites and the Hivites and the Jebusites, to a land flowing with milk and honey."' Then they will heed your voice; and you shall come, you and the elders of Israel, to the king of Egypt; and you shall say to him, 'The Lord God of the Hebrews has met with us; and now, please, let us go three days' journey into the

wilderness, that we may sacrifice to the Lord our God.' But I am sure that the king of Egypt will not let you go, no, not even by a mighty hand. So I will stretch out My hand and strike Egypt with all My wonders which I will do in its midst; and after that he will let you go. And I will give this people favor in the sight of the Egyptians; and it shall be, when you go, that you shall not go empty-handed. But every woman shall ask of her neighbor, namely, of her who dwells near her house, articles of silver, articles of gold, and clothing; and you shall put them on your sons and on your daughters. So you shall plunder the Egyptians." Exodus 3: 14 - 22

What a name – simply, "I Am." When God spoke His name, it transcended time. It told Moses and all others that God's authority has always been and would always be. It empowered Moses to know that God was not bound by time nor was His authority one that was sanctioned on Earth. It was and is a heavenly kingdom power.

God then told Moses to link this authority with the heritage and lineage of all those who trusted God before him. By Moses' identifying with Abraham, Isaac, and Jacob, the people of Israel would also join their faith with the generations of believers that came before. They were more likely to follow Moses and obey God by identifying themselves with their fathers in faith.

God assured Moses that He would be with Him. He gave Moses specific ways that He would be present with him, and told him how He would deliver them, plunder and confound the relentless authority and oppression of the Egyptians, and how He would lead them to a land that was theirs; one filled with overflowing blessing for generations to come.

This is a perfect story of how we can trust God and His provision, even when we doubt our own abilities. Moses' interaction with God shows me that I can doubt, but God's promise to carry me through will give me courage to follow and obey.

We Matter

Sometimes the demands of my husband and children (who needed constant resonance and love from me) overwhelmed me. The more they needed my attention, the more overwhelmed I felt; and the more overwhelmed I felt, the more I heard the voice of the enemy telling me, "You'll never be enough to meet these demands. You're a terrible wife and mother."

In those moments, I remembered the example of Moses. It was so easy to doubt my ability to accomplish such an impossible load and so easy to feel overwhelmed. But I recalled that by faith I could obey when I was strengthened by those who have gone before me, those who have heard and obeyed.

God used the overwhelming demands of my family to teach me not only the importance of hearing, but also the importance of being heard. Our relationship with Him is a conversation, a two way street, and He understands our need to be heard as well as our need to hear.

It was during those times of feeling overwhelmed that I learned some prioritizing techniques, techniques that seemed to quiet the voice of the enemy in my head.

First, I sought God to quiet my emotions. This brought a quiet response from the Holy Spirit, drowning out the accusations from the enemy. I heard Him gently and lovingly respond to my heart's cry; beckoning me to calmly tell the children to wait just a moment...be still for just that moment.

Secondly, I gave myself permission to go into another room or a different space for a moment of peace. When the demands of life with five kids became overwhelming, God often whispered for me to pull myself close to Him to find a space for quiet reflection.

"Oh God," I would pray, "Help me prioritize. Help me fight through the fog of frozen indecision and lift me into loving my children and others through meeting their needs. Help me to love them well. Help me resist emotions that make me want to react and be controlling. Help me listen well as their hearts need me to resonate with them right now."

God is so practical. As He calmed me, He spoke such practical wisdom to me. "Calm yourself. You are able to do each of these individual demands, aren't you? Try to meet the most important need first (definitely the diaper change and turn down the spaghetti). Then, look them in their sweet little faces (resonating with their hearts). Hear what they are saying (open your heart to hear behind the noise; to hear what they are actually not saying), and try to hear the whispers behind their voices and acknowledge that their hearts are aligned with yours. One by one, meet the needs of each child, without raging (bundling the overwhelming feelings into one), without using the anger of your fear to control."

And as I felt stronger, He spoke Truth to me. "The anger of the fear that 'you are not enough' is gone."

What a lesson for me and my pounding heart (and my throbbing ears)! God taught me that as much as I wanted to hear each one of my children, each one of them longed to be heard. Slowly, as I acknowledged their needs, repeated what they were asking me and got down on my knees in front of their sweet little faces, I could see that our hearts touched and that my overwhelmed feeling was overpowered by love. It was precious to see their hearts open when they realized I was hearing them, and I was listening to what mattered to them. When I was able to get down close to their faces, not be hurried to hear, the quiet and stillness rushed in. In those moments, one by one, all needs were taken care of, the children were truly heard, and we all learned an important lesson together - we matter.

Having a voice and really being heard, matters. When we don't feel heard, we feel afraid and out of control. Fear and control shuts down a heart. The fear of inadequacy projects into the hearts of others that their needs are too overwhelming to hear and be met. It tells them they are on their own to have their needs met, and alone in their need for love. When the enemy convinces us we do not matter, that we are alone and unloved, his voice becomes loud once again in our ears. As I have said before, Satan is a persistent schemer.

John 8:32 says, *"You will know the truth, and the truth will set you free."* When we draw near to God, when we learn to sit in His presence and recognize the sound of his voice, we become confident of this truth from His Word, *"How great is the love the father has lavished on us that we should be called the Children of God, and that is what we are."* This truth, and our deep understanding of it, will give us power to silence the voice of the enemy and to hear the whispers of God.

CHAPTER THREE:
SOUL MATES

*Learning to Draw Closer to God by
Drawing Closer to Our Spouse*

My love affair with my husband began when I was 15. We were in the same high school; he was one year ahead of me. I saw him one day from far off and immediately my heart leapt. His tall, rugged good looks were enough to grab any girl's attention, and did; but there was something deeper that caused my heart to wonder and my thoughts to wander toward him. His quiet strength demanded a response from me, and his presence in a group led me to his heart. There was something quite disconcerting about him when I was with him, as if I were experiencing a young man and not a young boy. It was as if he had already known about pain and life in similar ways that I had known them. It drew us to one another even though we were young in years, but obviously alike as we were quite old in our souls. I loved him the moment we met - the absolute moment.

Our story together the first year was like a movie; everywhere we went, I felt as if I were in a cinematic moment or a dream. I loved like I had never, ever, loved before. When he touched my hand, the shiver went down my arm straight to my heart. When we kissed, it was as if no one existed but us. When he called, I raced to answer the phone (you know, when the phones were still connected to the wall in places where everyone could always hear the conversations). I didn't care, though, because it was just the two of us, like no one else existed on the planet. The "I love you's" came easy; they fell off my tongue, and whenever I was going to see him, I couldn't be there fast enough. I had never loved like that before, and I will never love like that again. My heart was all in and all his.

We had our difficulties when he went to college a year ahead of me, the distance creating logistical issues for spending time together. We had distresses over commitments from being in two different locales and our hearts were longing to be together. His life story began to be less "our story" and more "his story," and for the first time, his need to belong somewhere, for friends and a sense of family, created discord between us. Because he had been truly abused and abandoned by his family of origin, he found himself alone and unsupported in a college atmosphere. It became difficult to keep his commitment to me with no transportation and with other commitments there. He lost his way to me and I to him.

We then separated and dated others. And though my heart was broken, I continued to love him even while we were in relationships with others. Those were superficial relationships; ones that filled the time and deepened my understanding that he was *the one*. We went on with the separation for two years until one day, quite providentially, he called me. He had been calling me periodically just to put in a heartfelt word that always left me sniveling and heartsick over what once was. This call, however, was different. Neither of us was dating anyone else, and because he told me he was unattached I got the idea late that night that I must go to Austin where he was. Come hell or high water I was going to go, only it would be under the guise of wanting to attend nursing school, which was not offered where I was currently attending. It might possibly give us another shot at being together.

After I transferred and was moved into my first University of Texas apartment, one day Don knocked on my door. There he stood in all his handsome, familiar tenderness and love. There he was after two excruciatingly long years. I stood amazed and loved him immediately again! Instantly! Thirty-nine years of marriage later, here we are.

For Better, For Worse

Lest you think my marriage has been this white picket-fenced dream, I will try my best to steer you toward truth and away from any delusions you might have. No one's marriage comes without challenges and trials, and mine has been no exception. My husband and I brought baggage loaded up, locked, and sealed from our lives prior to our marriage. Our lives before marriage were filled with dysfunctional ways to communicate, to handle pain, and to deal with "triggers" that would enrage or defeat us. Although our deep and abiding love for one another was evident, there were broken issues that surfaced as the years went by.

Don's childhood traumas resulted in him having PTSD, post-traumatic stress disorder. When he experienced scenarios that resembled his childhood, his reactions to that stress often came with rage and anger. My own triggers were based on victim-based mentalities and enabling co-dependencies. We should have been the history of our stories repeated, but mercifully, we were not. There was a deep commitment we shared to the commandments of God and to God Himself. That commitment came wrapped as the gift of love from Christ and deep abiding love for one another. It was cultivated in a deep respect and cherish for our marriage vows with God. It bound us together and pushed us toward healing and answers. It made us ever aware of the whispers of God in the middle of trauma. We'd fall down together and we'd get back up together. Our stories reflect redemption, healing and deep love.

One night, our son was in and out of bed, and after hours of prompting him back to bed, he got out of bed yet again. As my husband walked him back to his bed, something about the overwhelming responsibility and anger of dealing with a disruptive and disobedient behavior sent my husband into a rage. As I understand it now, rage is "bundled feelings." Instead of feeling sorrow, fear, loneliness, anger, or sadness, rage bundles many feelings together because of a lack of ability to cope with the feelings drawn out by certain "trigger" situations. It may seem, by those deeply wounded people like my husband, that rage will silence the feelings that are too painful to access. Rage pushes everyone out and speaks loudly to be left alone. Alone, as taught to me by the Whisperer, is the last place someone in pain should stay. Alone is where we begin to believe lies and we keep love away.

That night, my son happened to be the recipient of that kind of rage. My husband took the palms of his hands and pounded them on the sides of our little boy's bed. He raised his voice to a frightening pitch as he yelled my oldest son back under the covers. He was terrified. Both were terrified. My husband stomped out of the room, berating and saying hurtful things. As he left our son's room, tears streamed down my husband's face. He stomped into his bathroom and fell down on his floor and wept like I had never seen before. He admits now that he felt so alone. Tears were flowing and hearts were breaking. My son felt alone, I felt alone, and my husband felt alone. The lies we believed by being separated from each other in fear and anger were these:

> I am so unlovable.
> I am worth nothing.
> I am desperate and do not know what to do to make things better.
> I am alone.

The Whisperer then quietly told me to go get my son and go into the bathroom and pray. I got up, although feeling frozen in fear and hurt, and went and comforted my son. I told him that none of this overreaction was about him and how much he was loved. I told him that all parents make mistakes and have moments of lapsed judgment. I told him that I felt his pain and loved him. I told him that his father loved him very much. I held him tightly in my arms and let him cry. I asked him if he would like to go with me to pray for his dad, and he said yes. After making sure I had checked in with his feelings and that he had expressed his voice to me, I was led by the Holy Spirit to go into that bathroom and kneel down beside my weeping husband and pray. My seven-year-old, a very forgiving and loving son, and his younger brother knelt with me as we laid our hands on Don and prayed for his breaking heart. Years of bottled up emotion around abuse that Don suffered when he was a boy now faced him as he dealt with his little boy. I overrode my thought to become the victim, broken and hurt in my own right from rage that had been perpetrated on me as well. Frightened and weak, we approached Don's weeping, crumpled mess as he continued in sorrow over his actions. No words could fill the space where the hurt and healing poured out of him. We leaned in close and spoke words of forgiveness and love, understanding and acceptance.

Something else broke that night besides Don. Love was so thick in that room and in that place that fear and anger lifted. Abuse and rage had no power. Forgiveness and peace were ushered in. We all held each other until the pain subsided. We never forgot the leading of the whispers and the sweetness of the Holy Spirit. Forgiveness is an action. Love, too. God will always lead us, even in the middle of the most painful moments; He will lead us to love.

Perfect love casts out fear.

> *"There is no fear in love; but perfect love casts out fear..."* 1 John 4:18

A Prayer Wall

It's a long story, but to say my husband's love for Israel runs deep is an understatement. It was through his business partnerships with his friend, Isaac, as well as invitations to weddings, Bar Mitzvahs and Bat Mitzvahs, Feasts of Tabernacles, Passover celebrations, and the like, we have seen the Word of God actualized and made alive. It is truly a gift from God.

We had been invited to Isaac's daughter's Orthodox Jewish wedding, one of many Jewish celebrations we have been graciously included in as guests. When we first arrived at this massive hotel in Chicago, Don was whisked off to be with the men only, and I likewise went to be with the women. It terrified me to be alone and without Don. I was so fearful I might do something offensive or sacrilegious. As I was ushered into the room where the women were gathered, I glimpsed, for the first time, at the bride. As I sat in this large room, a stranger to most there, I watched an ancient prophetic drama unfold. The matriarchs of this family were doting over the bride. She sat peculiarly (to me) up on a platform in this room, with veil over her face, only to lift it when greeting the people coming in to see her. She continually was bowing her head as she held and was reading a little Bible (Torah) in a kind of genuflection in reverence to the Word of God. It reminded me of how we are to stay faithful in our knowledge of God's Word even as we patiently await His return. Her form was that of what you might imagine a true "virgin" to be: olive skin with large brown and beautiful eyes and a smile with lips described right out of Song of Solomon. She was waiting for her groom, patiently waiting, studying, longing, and preparing her heart with the Word of God.

I began to see and hear the whispers of the actualized and prophetic Word come to life. I saw the sweet picture of how I am called to prepare my heart for the return of Christ. The pure and unspotted bride awaiting her groom.

Then with a shout from the outer corridors of the hotel came the men, with laughter and praise, song and jubilation. The groom entered the room flanked on either side by his father and grandfather who were jubilantly and fervently praising God in Hebrew song. The bold and beautiful groom walked up to the platform to lift the veil on the face of his bride. You know the story; he lifts the veil to distinguish his bride just like Jacob did with Leah and Rachel. Then when her identity was confirmed, the procession began. First the men went into the room designated as the sanctuary for marriage. It was one that would take place under the chuppa, the tabernacle, tent-like structure placed in the middle of the hotel ballroom. The men were followed by the women, who were also praying while the bride's mother and grandmother were flanking both sides of this beautiful bride. As they approached the chuppa, the bride continued a march around her groom. She marched seven full circles around her betrothed, all while speaking the Word she was reading and while all the men were singing.

The scene conjured a feeling of deep joy and exhilarating tradition. I turned to a Jewish woman sitting near to me and asked what the bride was doing in this walk around her husband. She answered, "Why, she is building her prayer wall around her husband." And just like that – boom! - it hit me. The shout of His whisper to my longing heart, the Holy Spirit was speaking to me, whispering to my soul, "How's your prayer wall around Don?" I had to admit, "What prayer wall?" Was God, in His beautiful whisper, asking me to pray a wall around my husband? "What?" I said aloud in my spirit. I pray everyday, but a wall? A fortress? A position of strength and honor? A distinction of territory and kingdom? A gunnery against the wiles of his enemies? "Yes," He answered in His beautiful and resounding voice, and so I began to build.

From that night on, after Don was asleep, I laid my hands across his shoulders or on his head and prayed, asking God to reveal his needs to me. I asked Him what were some unspoken struggles Don was dealing with. I prayed for his peace and his healing and for his strength. God always met me there, just as He did when I went in to pray for my children. God met me there when I was too tired, when I felt far from God, when I was angry or even disappointed with Don, living in unforgiveness with a need to be right, or when I really didn't feel like praying because I, too, was needy or resentful, needing Don to nurture and care for me. But faithfully, God was always there to meet me in the quietness of His whisper. God revealed Don's needs in His beautiful and sweet way; His still, gentle, and small but reassuring voice that many times led me out of judgment of Don and into forgiveness with the realization of the very work God was also doing in me. That sweet time became a mirror for me to see all God also wanted to heal in me. As I prayed for Don, God was also healing me.

Just a side note, and by the way, it was while I was praying that Don thought I was rubbing his back. He would be half awake and think I was soothing him to sleep. He then began the nightly routine of asking me to "tickle his back" while he drifted to sleep. It's beautiful to know that the prayers were really the balm for us both.

Revelation 19:1-2, 7

"And I heard, as it were, the voice of a great multitude, as the sound of many waters and as the sound of mighty thunderings, saying, "Alleluia! For the Lord God Omnipotent reigns! Let us be glad and rejoice and give Him glory, for the marriage of the Lamb has come, and His wife has made herself ready."

I cannot help but link this Revelation passage to what I observed in that room at our friend's wedding. It's as if God were acting out this whole prophetic drama of Christ and His beautiful wedding feast so those who have eyes to see and ears to hear would be able to await His coming with expectant joy.

I remember hearing the loud, thunderous applause and shouts coming from the other room as the groom made His way to his bride. Jesus, too, as our bridegroom, will enter to receive us to Himself in a beautiful congregation of shouts and Alleluias. My hope can only be that I, His wife, His beloved, have made myself ready. Ready as that young virgin - spotless from the world, bowing in reverence to her reading of God's Word, and ever watchful for her groom's grand entrance while hearing His shout from the other side.

I see this:

> *"And to her it was granted to be arrayed in fine linen, clean and bright, for the fine linen is the righteous acts of the saints."* –Revelation 19:8

How we prepare to be ready for Jesus at any time depends greatly on our willingness to obey and hear His commands. Again He says, that to love Him is to keep His word. To be ready for the groom is to be granted the array of His linen garment. To be granted means to be gifted, delivered to, and freely bestowed upon. The garment is given freely to us in the authority of Christ Himself.

This passage shows us that the purity of righteousness from the white linen garment is clean and bright, just as that young olive-skinned bride awaited her groom in purity and righteousness. Like her, our garment is one of "fine" linen ONLY given to us because of Christ. We can only claim right standing before God because of the bestowment of Christ.

> *"But we are all like an unclean thing, and all our righteousnesses are like **filthy rags**."* Isaiah 64:6

In biblical terms, "fine linen" was reserved for the priests who spun their garments from both flax and wool. Flax represents the agricultural offering and wool represents the provision of sacrificial blood offering. How else could we expect God to make brides out of us except that He would infuse His covenant and sacrificial language into the very meaning of marriage? The "fine linen," in this prophetic word, tells us that the garment of Christ's bride is woven together as a priestly garment made from the "righteous acts of the saints" of God.

Righteousness to God is to be in right standing with Him. As we stand before Him, we are "right" with Him because of what our spotless Lamb, Christ, accomplished at the cross. Righteousness to our Jewish Jesus meant humility in spirit for the serving and giving to the poor.

These are ways that God calls us to be His: to prepare ourselves as His spotless bride, unspotted by the world, humble in our service to the poor, and in right standing with Him because of Jesus. He clothes us in His righteousness and we accept His ways as ours.

> *"Then he said to me, write: 'Blessed are those who are called to the marriage supper of the Lamb!'"*
> Revelation 19:9

John the Apostle is saying here that we are blessed in the invitation to that wedding feast with Him. We are blessed to be His bride clothed in fine linen as priests and kings who can stand before God and be in right standing before Him. We are blessed in the preparation of studying, hearing, and keeping the Word of God. We are blessed to celebrate with Him at the Marriage Feast of the Lamb.

CHAPTER FOUR:
BELIEVE ONLY

*Learning to Believe He Speaks
To Us and For Us*

The word was spreading about Jesus. People had physically seen the miracles He had performed and the news was spreading from person to person, village to village, and town to town. It had been 400 years since God had sent a prophet, so you can be sure when Jesus entered a new town, people showed up in droves.

I've often thought about the make-up of the crowds in Jesus' day. Surely there were scoffers, those who doubted He was the Son of God. And there would have been skeptics, those unsure that He was anything more than a magician with a new bag of tricks. And I imagine there were the open-minded lot, those who believed He *could be* the Son of God, but still, they needed to see things with their own eyes. And then there were those whose only hope was to believe He was who he said he was, the desperate, the sick, the lost, and the hopeless in despair.

Such was the crowd on the day that Jesus met Jairus as we read in Mark 5:21-24:

> *"Jesus went across the Sea of Galilee in a boat. It landed at the other side. There, a large crowd gathered around Him. Then a man named Jairus came. He was a synagogue ruler. Seeing Jesus, he fell at his feet. He begged Jesus, "Please come. My little daughter is dying. Place your hands on her to heal her. Then she will live." So Jesus went with him and a large crowd followed him and pressed in."*

Jairus was an incredibly important man. He could have sent for someone to bring Jesus to him, but Jairus was also a desperate father, one whose only hope in that moment was to believe that Jesus was who He said he was. He couldn't take the chance of sending someone else.

And although Jairus must have been in a great hurry to get Jesus back to where his daughter was, Jesus was not in a hurry. He was listening with His heart in the middle of a large and chaotic crowd. In the context of this passage, it is good to note that Jesus was on His way to Jairus' home when He stopped and took care of the woman who had been suffering with the issue of blood for many years. It was no trouble for him to take time to meet the needs of the people along the way, as if He carried with Him the whispering of His Father and the assurance that all would be taken care of in due time.

I'll be honest. If I were Jairus, I might have been tempted to hurry Jesus along. If it were my daughter's life on the line (and if I had the kind of authority Jairus had), I might have been moving the crowd out of the way and telling Jesus to get a move on. But Jesus was not in a hurry. He had time to wait and listen for his Father's voice as he walked among the crowd.

So often we are in a rush to push aside the needs of others. Sometimes it is because we are not willing to slow down to hear what the Father is saying. He is always with us even in the middle of chaotic scenarios. Sometimes we rush hearing the needs of others because we selfishly center our lives around our own needs. Jesus is calling us to slow down, stop what we are doing, listen to His small, quiet voice, and "believe only" that all is in His control, not ours. Peace will rush in. As it says in scripture, "The work of righteousness will be peace; the effect of righteousness, quietness and assuredness forever." Isaiah 32:17

Believe Only

As Jesus was healing and speaking to the woman with the issue of blood, we read this:

> *"While he yet spoke, there came one from the ruler of the synagogue's house, saying to him (Jairus), Thy daughter is dead; trouble not the Master."* Mark 5:49

Jairus' daughter was dead. There was no longer a need for Jesus to come.

> *"But when Jesus heard it, he answered him, saying, Fear not: believe only, and she shall be made whole."* Mark 5:50

Jesus said to Jairus, "Believe only." Only what? "Believe only" against fear and doubt? "Believe only" that Jesus can raise her even if she is dead? "Believe only" when thoughts come rushing in blaming Jesus for not going at a faster pace?

> *"And when he came into the house, he suffered (prevented) no man to go in, save Peter, and James, and John, and the father and the mother of the maiden. And all wept, and bewailed her: but he said, Weep not; she is not dead, but sleeps."*
> Mark 5:51-52

Notice the people that Jesus allowed to go in with him? A few disciples and the father and mother of the little girl. Perhaps they were the only ones there with the necessary faith to "believe only," even though the natural eye may have believed something else.

> *"Now, faith is the substance of things hoped for and the evidence of things not seen."* Hebrews 11:1

> *"And they laughed him to scorn, knowing that she was dead. And he put them all out,"* – Mark 5:53-54

Other than those few faithful individuals, Jesus wanted everyone out of the room who mocked and scorned, as if their presence in that scenario hindered the work of healing in that space. Doubt and living in a world where what we see is only that with our natural eyes is not the space God occupies. He wants us to see and hear with our supernatural eyes and ears, ones that are finely tuned to the rhythms of His ways and His kingdom.

Jesus even prophesied that she was not dead but sleeping. She was most certainly dead in the natural sense, so what was Jesus implying? People of that day knew how to determine if she were dead or alive. Jesus peeled back the veil of what separated the natural from the supernatural and heard his Father and Holy Spirit speak life to the child. It was Jesus' faith joined with certain disciples and Jairus to "believe only" that ultimately healed her.

> "And (He) took her by the hand, and called, saying, Maid, arise." And her spirit came again, and she arose straightway: and he commanded to give her meat. And her parents were astonished ..." Mark 5:56-58

The little girl heard the voice of Jesus, and she arose.

There are times in our lives when we know God is asking us to "believe only." The faith to "believe only" is a mighty faith. It comes from having seen what God can do. It comes from needing to desperately believe He can do what He promises. And sometimes the faith to "believe only" comes from hearing and obeying His voice.

Do You Need Help?

One Sunday, while attending church in Houston, I noticed a large family sitting about two rows ahead of where we were sitting. There sat a mom, dad, young teenage girl, two younger siblings, and an infant. The mom at the edge of the row was holding the infant trying her best to keep the baby from interrupting the speaker. As she failed at the bumping and patting, she passed the infant down the line to enlist the help of anyone else in the family, but especially the help of her teenage daughter. I kept feeling my gaze travel back toward them. I watched them as they participated in the offering and the Sunday morning routine, as most families were doing the same. But something would not let me look away.

My heart began to swell with something as I continued to watch. The pastor asked if anyone needed prayer, and I found myself praying for them. I did not know why; but I could hear a slight resonance in my heart for them, like a small voice of the Father trying to soften my heart toward them. For the life of me I did not know why.

When the service was over and it was time to leave, we went home but that family took over a little space in my heart, coming to mind throughout the day. I figured I was to keep praying for them, so I did.

The following Sunday came, and we sat in our usual places in the long pew at church. After I had settled all my children in their places, pulled out all the pencils, crayons, sticker books, Bibles, and papers, I looked up and saw that seated two rows in front of me was that same family. This time, maybe because I had been praying for them, my heart jumped a bit when I saw them. This time when there was a call to prayer, I prayed and found myself praying specifically for them. Then, out of nowhere, I heard this small voice. "Ask her (the young girl) if she needs help taking care of her baby." "What?!?" I thought. "That's not her baby. She's just a young girl herself." I heard it again and then a third time. I quickly put it out of my mind and prayed as usual and found myself walking out of service with a heavy pull in my heart.

All day long, all week long, when I was cleaning, when I was helping my own five children, when I was washing dishes, when I was cooking, I found my heart drifting toward that young girl and that precious baby. I could not stop hearing that whisper in my soul, "Ask her if she needs help taking care of her baby." I found myself arguing with the voice in my head, "What if that is not her baby, and he is her little brother? What if I offend her by asking? What if she thinks I'm crazy?" Of course, by this time I thought I just might be crazy. The directive now followed me wherever I was. I was even awakened on numerous occasions with the question fermenting in my heart. "Do you need help with your child?" I realized with great trepidation that if I asked the question, I surely had some reasonable responsibility to be the one to help. "But God, I just finished potty training my last child of five. I cannot possibly take an infant on the runs I make with five children to the store, to soccer practice, to school, to cheerleading, to, you name it. I couldn't possibly have the strength to even try." My argument fell on deaf ears. The question resonated louder and with more fervor. It got to the point that if I did not ask her, I would not be able to stand it.

Six weeks later (I know, I am stubborn), as we were leaving church, I was gathering coats and looking for anything we had left behind. The children were walking out with their father. As I was shuffling behind the crowd and down the aisle, I looked up, my arms draped with four or five coats and sweaters, as well as all the paper and pencils my brood had left behind. I slowly, almost as if in slow motion, lifted my gaze and there was the young woman standing shoulder to shoulder with me filing out of church along with the 7,000 other people there. She was so close to me, I could have touched her shoulder. I heard God say, "Is that clear enough for you? Is that confirmation enough? She's as close as a touch. Ask her. Ask her now."

I reached out and lightly touched her shoulder. My hands and heart were trembling. I said, "Excuse me. Could you come out into the front with me? I need to ask you something?" She looked into my eyes and with some questions in hers said she would. There we were face to face. I had been praying for her for all these weeks. I didn't know if the baby was hers. I didn't know if she needed help. I didn't know anything but that whisper in my heart telling me to ask, "Do you need help?" I said, "I am so sorry to bother you. You do not know me, but I have been praying for you for about six weeks, and I have not been able to get you off my mind and out of my heart." My eyes were welling up with tears. She smiled but looked at me with a confused look in her eyes. I continued, "I have been praying for you, and I believe with all my heart, no matter how awkward this seems, that I am supposed to ask you if you need me to help you with your baby?"

She gasped and then the tears began to stream down her flushed cheeks and she couldn't speak. She asked me to repeat what I had said. When I did, she asked me to wait right where I was standing. She sprinted down the hall and grabbed the woman I had first thought was the mother of the infant. She was actually holding the infant as they both returned to where I was. The young girl asked me to repeat what I had said after she had introduced me to her mother. When I told her what was on my heart, they both were crying. The young girl explained, "You see, the baby is mine. I am nineteen years old, and I am not married. My parents have helped me so far, but I cannot even leave the house to find a way to support my child because my mother is working two jobs now, and my father is deaf and cannot work. I have been desperately trying to find an answer for us, but I cannot afford someone to watch my baby, and I cannot leave him with my dad. What you are offering is an answer to my prayers. I cannot believe this because I have been hopelessly resolved that I might have to give him up for adoption, but me and my parents want him to stay in our family. I love him so much but I need help. I cannot even afford diapers and formula. I cannot leave to find work. Oh my, oh my!"

The tears were flowing, and they agreed to come to my house to sit down and work out the details. When they came, they were overwhelmed by the love of the Father. I was too especially that He would speak so very specifically. We just sat and cried and realized together that His ways were higher than ours. Who were we to ever question? I realized how intimately my Father had spoken to me; and how He led me with a whisper.

I kept little Austin for over a year while they got back on their feet. Mama got a job and was able to afford care for him. I was able to help her with some nutritional needs Austin had, and his health improved as well. Austin's grandparents got to watch him grow into a precious little boy. His mama got into a young person's Sunday school class and connected with people her own age. Eventually she was able to move out of her parents' home and make her life work.

I can't help but think that in the midst of her heartache, while God was telling me, "Ask her, 'Do you need help?'" He was telling her, "Believe only." God was speaking *to* me, *for* her. I was forever changed, and you can be sure I listened and obeyed much more quickly after that.

There is a Purpose

Hannah was a young woman who found herself wanting a child. For years she had been treated bitterly by her husband's other wife who had taunted Hannah over her inability to conceive. One evening, while at the temple, Hannah was in prayer and made a vow to God that if He gave her a child, her son would be on loan and in service to the Lord forever. Watching her anguished prayer, the priest, Eli, prayed for her, asking God to give her a child. And the Lord did just that.

When Samuel was old enough, Hannah did as she vowed and took him, her only child, to live with Eli, the Chief Priest. I cannot imagine the strength of character it took for this woman to give over her only child after years of barrenness and being taunted by her husband's other wife. But Hannah "believed only" that God had a purpose for Samuel's life. And He did.

> *"But Samuel ministered before the Lord, even as a child, wearing a linen ephod. Moreover his mother used to make him a little robe, and bring it to him year by year when she came up with her husband to offer the yearly sacrifice. And Eli would bless Elkanah and his wife, and say, "The Lord will give you descendants from this woman for the loan that was given to the Lord." Then they would go to their own home. And the Lord visited Hannah, so that she conceived and bore three sons and two daughters. Meanwhile the child Samuel grew before the Lord."* 1 Samuel 2: 18 - 21

It is beautiful to see Hannah fulfilled her promise to the Lord and that God not only blessed her obedience with Samuel, but with other children as well. Hannah did not waver from her obedience to God's will. And God did, indeed, have a purpose for Samuel's life.

> *"So Samuel grew, and the Lord was with him and let none of his words fall to the ground. And all Israel from Dan to Beersheba knew that Samuel had been established as a prophet of the Lord. Then the Lord appeared again in Shiloh. For the Lord revealed Himself to Samuel in Shiloh by the word of the Lord."* 1 Samuel 3:19-21

God delivered the children of Israel from the evil and wicked generations of Eli and his sons. He did so by raising up Samuel as His mouthpiece, His prophet. A prophet is one who hears from God and then shares that word with the people of God. Samuel's destiny was prepared for him before he was ever born. Through his obedience and the obedience of his mother, the whole nation of Israel saw redemption and deliverance. God spoke *to* Hannah, and He spoke *through* Samuel, and He did so *for* the people of Israel.

Like Hannah and Samuel, we must learn to believe God speaks to us for our good and the good of others. While we might not understand His plans or His purpose, as we become more and more accustomed to the sound of His voice, and we become more and more obedient to His call on our life, we will fulfill the purpose He has for us on this earth.

CHAPTER FIVE:
DEEP CALLS TO DEEP
*Learning to Follow God's Voice
Wherever He Leads*

"Then He said, "Go out, and stand on the mountain before the LORD." And behold, the LORD passed by, and a great and strong wind tore into the mountains and broke the rocks in pieces before the LORD, but the LORD was not in the wind; and after the wind an earthquake, but the LORD was not in the earthquake; and after the earthquake a fire, but the LORD was not in the fire; and after the fire a still small voice." I Kings 19:11-12

Ears To Hear

My husband, Don, and I were praying as we felt a season of change approaching. I don't know how we could tell, but we knew it was coming. We attributed it to the work of the Holy Spirit, who was speaking to us in our quiet times, in our prayers, and in all the teachings we were hearing at church and on Christian radio. As we sought counsel and wisdom from our friends and teachers, the still, small voice of God spoke to us in a beckoning way, calling us into something that seemed was a missing component in our lives. We knew it was coming, but did not know what impact this change would have in our lives.

Our family life was deeply engrained in our church life. My children and I had friends there, my husband taught at the Sunday school there, and we were surrounded by deep and beautiful believers. Not only that, my children attended the school that was run by our church, one of the finest private Christian schools in the Houston area. As I was talking with some friends there, I heard about a home school conference that was to be hosted in our area. And though I had no need for a home school, I decided I would attend.

Once at the conference, I made my way around to all of the curricula tables, and I visited with all of the people who were selling their home school materials. I got to the end of the displays, and at the very last table I visited, there was a sweet-hearted woman presenting her books. She asked, "How long have you been home schooling?" I replied quickly and with great confidence, "Oh, I don't home school;my children go to a beautiful Christian school. I don't really know why I am even here!" Her eyes caught mine, and she slowly looked up with the tenderness and all the love she could muster and said, "Uh-oh. You should be very ready then. I was in your same position about seven years ago. I had no need for home schooling and went to a conference much like this one. I said those exact words you just said to me. I didn't know why I was there. Three months later, my husband was moved to a remote location where we knew no one, and I then learned everything I needed to know about home schooling. I have been doing it ever since." Filled with fear and denial, I thought, "This has zero application to me."

By this time, because of a series of God-ordained events, my husband was selling his business at the Port of Houston. There had been so many confirmations this was what God was doing, we simply could not deny it. As God's beckoning grew louder, and clearer as the months passed by, and because our hearts were drawing closer to Him, we began to see confirmation signs that God was indeed moving us toward a major change.

At the same time, we were learning from Henry Blackaby's book, *Experiencing God*. In it, he challenged the believer to see what God was doing in their lives and to join Him. It was a simple but profound building block for Don and me to grasp. Through it we learned to open our eyes to the obvious leadings of the Holy Spirit. We learned to recognize God's voice and more importantly how to obey when called.

In John 5:19, Jesus says, *"Truly, truly, I say to you, the Son can do nothing of Himself, unless it is something He sees the Father doing; for whatever the Father does, these things the Son also does in like manner."* I imagine Jesus walking along, ear pressed to heaven, following this way and that, listening to the inseparable Word of God. "Do I go here? Do I go there? Do I enter into Zaccheus' home; rush to Jairus' daughter? How quickly do I leave to heal my friend, Lazarus, or must I remain here awhile more for the woman with the issue of blood? Not My will, but Thine, dear Father."

We pondered these truths deep in our hearts and began practicing the presence of the Spirit, by listening and obeying. We read books of similar titles and soaked in "The Practice of the Presence of God," by Brother Lawrence in his monastic journals.

"Having found in many books different methods of going to God, and diverse practices of the spiritual life, I thought this would serve rather to puzzle me than to facilitate what I sought after, which was nothing but how to become wholly God's...because we can do nothing without Him...it also begets a holy freedom, and if I may speak, a familiarity with God, wherewith we ask, and that successfully, the graces we stand in need of. In fine, by often repeating

these acts, they become habitual, and the presence of God rendered as it were natural to us."[4]

In learning to see and practice the presence of God, our hearts and minds become increasingly attuned to His will and to the sound of His voice. The more we heard His voice, the more we slowed our lives, until eventually His voice was an ever-present part of us.

> *"Stillness should be this low hum in the background like the waft of the aroma of apple pie in the house."*
> **Pastor Jamie George, Journey Church Franklin, TN**

SH'MA: Hear and Come Follow Me

We were invited by my family to spend a long weekend at their place in the country. Don informed me as we were planning to go for part of our Spring Break with the kids that he felt led by God to stay home, to pray and fast, and to study God's Word, as this call increased its pull on our hearts. We knew there was to be a change, but as I said earlier, we did not know what. Was it related to the selling of the business? Was it a total change in career? We had so many friends, after hearing Don teach our hundred-plus capacity Sunday school class, telling him he needed to go to seminary and to be a pastor. Was this the change? Was it a move?

Don even wrestled with a fear that God would eventually make him poor again like he had been as a child. But even with that fear, Don was changed. He wanted God to call him to do anything that changed his desires to become more like God's. We had more questions, and needed more prayer. We were drawing nearer to God than we had ever been before. We sought His presence in everything we considered, seeking only His voice.

---

4 Lawrence, Brother. The Practice of the Presence of God. Springdale, PA.: Whitaker House, 1982. 31-32.

We had already risked, changed, and lost significant relationships with family and friends because of our expressed faith. Yet, we could sense His hand on our lives in such real time and all we wanted to do was press in deeper and stronger. We didn't really know what that looked like, but our hearts longed for a deeper knowledge of Him.

> *"Draw near to God and He will draw near to you."* – James 4:8

Don stayed home, but I was filled with much anticipation. I called him every few hours to see what he was experiencing. My calls were mostly disappointing as his report was filled with the quietness that had drawn him in. There was nothing much to tell me in the first few days. He had read and studied books by Derek Prince titled *Fasting* and *Shaping History through Prayer and Fasting*. It helped him practically in his days of seeking God.

One last day I called him and asked, "How's it going for you? Any answers or direction from God?" There was silence on the phone. He told me that he believed God *had* spoken to him and he was anxious for me to come home so he could share some insights with me face to face. "Okay," I thought. "Great." I found myself looking forward to long talks of what God had shown him. Don had always sought God for answers for healing of his past wounds. He was in constant search for the answers to why his heart was so damaged and was tightly closed in some areas. This seemed different, as if these answers were answers to a call on his life, a call to greater service. Somehow that service and dependence on God was going to be part of his healing. It would be pieces of puzzles coming together in an undeniable way. Heaven only knew of it all.

One night while Don was praying, he saw a picture in the eyes of his heart what most would call a vision. He had never experienced anything of the sort before and although it was a new communication vehicle, he knew it was from God. In his vision, he saw this:

- A little town.
- One main street with a post office at one end
- A school in the middle and an office for rent
- On the other side of the street
- In the mountains
- Seemed to be Colorado

From that vision, and what appeared to us to be a call from God, we set out to discover confirmations. We drove to Colorado on several occasions and two of those times with all five children in tow. We stopped and prayed along the way, staying in an eclectic collection of motels and hotels. In between the treks across country, dear friends as well as some random people heard what we were doing and would call with the most specific prayers from what they believed to be from God. We had one friend put us in touch with what ended up being "The Navigators" in Colorado Springs. They offered Don a job almost immediately, but the whisper was silent. It did not seem like that was quite where we were supposed to be.

Perhaps our inability to discern might have been competing with the extremely loud voice of our scared and confused daughter who did not believe that God could be calling us away from Houston. I think her pain from that experience and loss still stays with her to this day. Our deep regret is that we may not have handled her grief in the best and most sensitive way. In retrospect, as we recognized our need to stay strong to hear God, we may not have given as much room for her voice too. I remember thinking, "Oh my, we will make a ruin of her life. She will never know how to trust God because she is only thirteen and at a time where her friendships and life are on the precipice." I was terrified we were making a mistake. I think there was a special fear concerning her as we might have to face and acknowledge our own failure as parents, sooner rather than later. Our greatest difficulty came in balancing what we knew to be God's whisper to us and our fears related to our daughter.

It turned out that after I had pleaded with God to sell our house quickly, almost to prove it was actually His call and not some wild dream we had, the first person that walked into our home bought it. But strangely, they did not want to close for nine months. The nine-month date was exactly the last day of our upset daughter's commitment as head cheerleader. She had enjoyed that honor with her lifelong best friend, and she was devastated to leave. I cried and wrestled with God about how that decision might hurt her for life, but believed that His love for her was proven in the timing of the move. I could only hold onto the thread of faith in that quiet and calming voice that reassured me daily in prayer that she would be blessed in our obedience. I was broken, as I knew her pain. I was relying on God to prove that we were hearing from Him and she would be okay. I was so afraid I might turn her away from Him instead of leading her to Him.

While we were trying to find out what God had in store for us, and where He wanted us to go, we were in a little motel somewhere near Colorado Springs. We were like a band of searchers, nomads listening for God in job offer after job offer, church after church, town after town, all the while trying to justify to our kids and to ourselves what this crazy journey was all about. We had traveled to Colorado plenty with our family, but had always flown into and then back out again, never really understanding relative proximities of one town to another. Mostly we had traveled to Aspen for skiing or summer visits, never realizing what, if any, towns were close by.

Early in our nomad days, my son had grabbed about fifteen travel brochures off of a tourist brochure rack, all places to visit in Colorado. As we prayed together with our little family, my son, Tillman, flung those brochures across the foldout bed. He pointed to the little town of Glenwood Springs and said to his dad, "What about this town? It looks like what your vision was like." We looked at the brochure and thought it was as good a place as any and decided we would drive there first thing in the morning.

This was the last place we were going to visit on this trip, and we were to be leaving the towns of Colorado Springs, Pueblo, and Boulder. On the way to Glenwood Springs, Don called the Chamber of Commerce and asked,"Is there a post office on Main Street? Right down from that is there a school? Across the street from those, is there office space to lease?" The answer to all three questions was simply," Yes."

We were pondering that answer because nowhere else we had been had proven his vision to be true. We drove into Glenwood Springs weary and discouraged and after having met people from churches, Navigators and Campus Crusades for possible ministry opportunities, none seemed a fit. We saw the office space, the post office, and the school and stayed there with our children on what to us all seemed like a nice vacation time together. We prayed, discussed, and prayed some more, but we were waiting for that whisper, a sense that all was right.

It was time to return to Houston, and Don and I decided we would return one more time to see if God would confirm that Glenwood Springs would be our new home. Because we had sold our house, people knew we were planning to move, but we could not tell them exactly where. We were waiting for God's voice. It was difficult, as we seemed like fools in the wisdom of rational thought. We could hear God's encouragements to keep waiting and listening. It was an incredible, fearful, questioning, and exciting time of faith for us all. My daughter reminded me that she was "NOT hearing from God and was not going." My dear sons could think of nothing but the beautiful wildlife, outdoor escapades, and fun-filled adventures. My other youngest two clung to me in the excitement of the travel easy and resilient.

Faith Is The Great Counterweight To Fear

Don and I then scheduled one more trip, just the two of us, back to Glenwood Springs. We walked around. We looked at property. We looked at the schools. We visited churches. Something was still left unsaid and unheard. We were trusting God and fine-tuning our hearts, but I had a deep sense of the need for Christian education for my kids. They went to the beautiful *Second Baptist Christian Academy* in Houston, and I wanted that educational opportunity to continue for them. So, we went to talk to a pastor at a local church in Glenwood. Oh, how our lives can change in a moment, in just a twinkling.

We sat down with him in his office. We asked him a myriad of questions about the life there and the life in faith there. Then, I asked him if there were any Christian schools in the area. He asked us to wait a moment, and he pulled out a sheet of paper with the names of about twelve Christian schools in the area. What we didn't know about the area at the time was that a valley was comprised of four separate communities and although they were autonomous, they were also interconnected. They all shared services like bus systems, schools, Wal-Mart, and shopping.

While reading this list, I noticed Lutheran preschools, Catholic day care, and one little school that just jumped off the page. I didn't know why, but I needed to know more about this school, *Alpine Christian Academy*. I can still feel the tingling in my heart when I saw its name. I asked the pastor more about it, and he said it was a new school located just up-valley from there. He gave us their number and when I returned to the car we called them.

A woman answered the phone with a pleasant and gracious demeanor. I found myself accepting her invitation to travel about 15 miles to come visit the little school. We packed up and went to see. As we walked into the little house, there were children sharing headphones with what appeared to be two to three grade levels and also sharing space in one room. The headphones were used with grade level DVD's with teachers for grades K-5th. I was greeted with smiles and the most polite and warm welcome I had ever received from children. They showed me their work, and I was able to sense the spirit of what they were doing. It touched my heart so deeply.

I heard this quiet voice in my heart. "This is it. This is what you've been waiting to see." The Holy Spirit was beckoning me in that place, and it almost overwhelmed me. I was listening. I had tears in my eyes as we left one of the sweetest experiences I had ever had. Although a stark contrast to the school we were leaving; I knew it was God. It is difficult to logically explain, but I knew it was His voice leading. When we were leaving, the headmistress asked if I might like to come to their church that evening for a prayer gathering for women. I was grateful and accepted her hospitality.

Don and I walked down the street of that little town and sat down in a café to share a pastry and some tea. Don was seated across from me and was facing out toward the street. While we were visiting and talking about how the 15 mile drive from Glenwood would not be bad for the children to go to school, I looked up into Don's face. Big tears were in his eyes, streaming down his cheeks and he grabbed my hand and led me to the sidewalk outside. He said, "This is it. This is my vision." He continued, "We walked from the school, past the post office and look, look, there's an office for rent right there across the street. This is the vision God gave me." We both wept. We knew we were supposed to go back to Glenwood, pack our things from the hotel there, and come down to this little town of Basalt, Colorado. We walked around and found out from locals there was a bed and breakfast with a room ready and available for the remainder of our time.

I was reticent to go to the evening prayer time with the ladies from the church, but I reluctantly went. I was so incredibly thankful I did go as each woman there prayed for me and sweetly welcomed me. I felt as if I had just gotten home from a long journey and that God was leading me by His faithful whispers. It was the sweetest time. I thought in my heart, "This is where He is leading us."

When I returned, I found Don in deep conversation with the owners of the bed and breakfast. Remember his love for Israel? Well, they were both Messianic Jews who belonged to this same church where I had shared prayer. They stayed up all night discussing Jesus, the Messianic movement, and their mutual love for Israel. The confirmed voice of God through His spirit was undeniable. The doors and opportunities were opening us to new and beautiful relationships. Don would later become the pastor of that church and go to Israel many times with sweet believers. The love for Israel was a deep legacy that had been planted in this little church in the mountains of Colorado. It was a rare gem, and God had led us to this place where all of our heart's longings were being revealed.

Our time in Basalt became some of the sweetest years for our family. My reluctant daughter developed an even deeper, more personal relationship with God and served as a mission worker in El Salvador and Africa. She had seen the hand of God hold her in Houston then release her at the exact time her commitment as cheerleader was complete. On that point I would hang, and lead her to the knowledge that God had her desires specifically in His hands. It built our faith. She met her precious husband because of that move. She testifies that the faith we all relied on soon was personalized for her.

Obedience Brings Blessing

We have all seen the hand of God when we heard Him say, "Come, follow me." We laid down everything we knew to be safe and secure to follow the whisper of God's leading. We had been in a place of comfortable Christianity, one that demanded little of us to believe on the edge of what was seen and unseen, spoken, heard and unheard. The move proved to bring great blessing, a real stretching of who we all realized God to be. I learned to hear God in a completely new and amazing way. I learned to trust Him even when I could not see and when it seemed dark and frightening. I learned to trust Him when the enemy was shouting in my other ear that my child's heart was being broken in the process. Through all of this, my heart has never been the same.

My sweet daughter who struggled with this move ended this part of her story with her own personal relationship with Jesus strengthened and fortified. It was later there she met the love of her life and served short-term missions in Botswana, Africa, and El Salvador. Although I had been reticent before, I did end up home schooling most of my children; some through high school graduation. My sister and husband followed us to Basalt and after fifteen years of our prayer for them, they came to know the Lord. My brother-in-law became the headmaster of our little Christian School. Our lives were never the same. We never know what the layers of work God might be doing that hinges on our simple hearing and obedience-Sh'ma lived out. He is in the business of changing hearts and lives.

When God Says Go

We were inspired by the story of Abraham. He heard God. He obeyed. He was blessed. Read it with me in Genesis 12.

> *"Now the Lord had said to Abram: "Get out of your country, From your family And from your father's house, To a land that I will show you. I will make you a great nation; I will bless you And make your name great; And you shall be a blessing. I will bless those who bless you, And I will curse him who curses you; And in you all the families of the earth shall be blessed."* Genesis 12: 1-3

God spoke to Abram. He listened and heard Him say to move far from the land he was from. He was to go to a land that was promised him by God. He was to leave before he knew where God was taking him. The reason was unclear to Abram who would later, because of his obedience, be given a new name, a heavenly name that identified Abraham to God. Sarai, his wife, too, would receive a blessed new name from God and would be called Sarah. They left, not knowing anything but that God had told them to "go."

My goodness, could we relate? We knew God had a plan for us. We knew we were hearing his voice correctly, and like His promise to Abraham, we knew we would experience His blessing. But first, we had to go. When we went, like Abram and Sarai, God also gave us our new identities, new names and purposes. We might never have known the depth of His great plan and love for us, had we not listened and obeyed.

> *"Then the Lord appeared to Abram and said, 'To your descendants I will give this land.'" And there he built an altar to the Lord, who had appeared to him. And he moved from there to the mountain east of Bethel, and he pitched his tent with Bethel on the west and Ai on the east; there he built an altar to the Lord and called on the name of the Lord. So Abram journeyed, going on still toward the South."* Genesis 12:7 - 9

God knew they were in want of a son. They were seventy years old when they left and yet later we see that God promises an inheritance of children as a blessing to Abraham that would outnumber the stars in the heavens and the sands in the seas. How could this impossible promise be true?

Let's read on in Genesis 15:

> *"After these things the word of the Lord came to Abram in a vision, saying, "Do not be afraid, Abram. I am your shield, your exceedingly great reward." Then Abram said, "Look, You have given me no offspring; indeed one born in my house is my heir!" And behold, the word of the Lord came to him, saying, "This one shall not be your heir, but one who will come from your own body shall be your heir." Then He brought him outside and said, "Look now toward heaven, and count the stars if you are able to number them." And He said to him, "So shall your descendants be." And he believed in the Lord, and He accounted it to him for righteousness. Then He said to him, "I am the Lord, who brought you out of Ur of the Chaldeans, to give you this land to inherit it."* Genesis 15: 2-7

Again, God declares Himself as "I Am." He also says He is Abraham's great reward. How often do I miss that my reward is Him and only Him? The things of this world that my heart desires pale in comparison to my true inheritance in Christ. How often must I stop to be grateful that it is only in Christ that I receive my true blessing? His reward to me is Himself. I see in Abraham's life the fear that he will never see the fruits of children and he questions God. Fear supplants faith and keeps building its wall around our hearts. I, too, remember that sense of fear, when I couldn't see how God could work all those things together for good, but I trusted Him. We trusted Him, and when God said, "Go," we went. Just like Abraham. When we truly take God at His word, and "only believe", His power of blessing and life are manifest in us. As we know Abraham to be the Father of our faith, the father of the Nation of Israel and the lineage from Israel by which the Messiah, Christ came, we see that God is faithful, trustworthy, and worthy of our praise.

CHAPTER SIX:
OPEN DOORS
Learning to Hear God's Voice in Unforeseen Places

There are many times in our lives where God speaks to us in unconventional ways and in unforeseen places. Perhaps it's through a chance encounter with a stranger or a message we see on a billboard. Maybe it's through a song (very often that is the case with me) or set of circumstances that happen in our lives. I have often heard people say they heard God's voice when he closed doors to certain opportunities they were considering. I have also often heard people say they have heard God speak through doors that he opened. Very often it's when we least expect to hear God's voice at all that we hear it the loudest.

A Signing Bonus

My father, Bud, was an All-American defensive lineman and offensive guard. He played for The University of Texas in the late 1940's, where he met and married his beauty queen and campus sweetheart, Betty. Betty and Bud shared a deep and passionate love for one another in their years there. By the look on my mother's face in every picture of the two of them together, she seemed to adore the very ground upon which he walked. His image portrayed a cuddly bear of comfort mixed with handsome self-assuredness and a quiet tenderness toward my mother. Both were quite the handsome couple; a couple whose presence made an impact when they walked into a room. Even 50 years later, Betty and Bud were remembered as the campus darlings by the secretary in the Athletic Director's office.

But that charming, handsome couple was not the couple I grew up with. Bud, the All-American, left us when I was five years old. His leaving created a domino effect on a lady who was once the beauty and belle of the ball of life, and it contributed to the broken-hearted, alcoholic, wreck–of-a-life that became the picture of my mother. When she looked outside she saw a gray world. She never quite recovered from the loss of my dad and eventually died from an overdose of pills and alcohol. I blamed my dad, and in the midst of grieving my mom's loss, I grieved the loss of him in my life all as well.

Fast forward to many years later:

My son, Tillman, was a high school sophomore and junior in the early 2000's. He was an, All-American and was actively recruited by Washington, Colorado, Stanford, Colorado State, to name just a few. You would have thought that The University of Texas would have been after him, but we did not live in that region of the country anymore and with Nebraska and Michigan just finishing the season in a shared number one position, Tillman's sights were set on playing for Nebraska.

When Tillman attended the football camp at Nebraska, and Tom Osborne walked up to him after practice one day and offered him a full-ride scholarship to the University of Nebraska, you would have thought Tillman could have answered right on the spot, no questions asked. It was his dream. Coach Osborne said, "Son, how does it feel to be offered a full-ride to the number one football school in the nation?" Tillman answered, "It's my dream come true, Coach, and I am truly happy. Thank you so much." And, that was that. We all assumed we would be sporting red and cheering "Go Big Red" for the Huskers for the next four years.

When Tillman got back home, he was thrilled, of course, but said he was not quite ready to commit to Nebraska. His dad and I were a bit confused but trusted his desire to wait. Months went by and the Nebraska staff called him at least twice a week for weeks on end. Ron Brown, a Godly man and coach at Nebraska, called him more than any other. His love and influence for Tillman was evident. It made us feel safe about Nebraska as a choice for our son. Finally, his dad said to him, "Tillman, this is getting a little awkward and here's why, son. It's like Nebraska has asked you to marry them and you keep saying that you'll have to get back with them. It's time to commit."

Tillman knew a lot was on the line and yet he kept saying he did not have complete peace about his decision. I, of course, wanted the agonizing to stop and didn't fully understand the delay to fulfill what we all knew was his dream. But he kept saying he was waiting for a peace from God. He was waiting for God to speak directly to him about it. It seems now, as I look back, he was waiting for that still, quiet whisper. You would have thought we would have been thrilled that he was waiting to see what God thought about the situation. After all, we had truly wanted our children to hear from God and to have their own unique relationship with Him.

The world, including us, was shouting all around him, "Nebraska! Nebraska!" He says now, after a lifetime of trying to hear God's voice in difficulties, "many times the whisper of God is louder than the shout from the world around us." So he waited. We all thought he was going to lose the offer. We wondered if he was just scared. We thought he might be changing his mind altogether. He just kept saying, "I am waiting to hear from God. I do not yet have the peace I need."

One evening, we were all meeting up at our dear friend's home for a FCA (Fellowship of Christian Athletes) gathering. Under pressure from everyone, he had decided he would call the coach at Nebraska and go ahead and commit. He did not seem sure, but he was also trying to listen to the people around him. This would be the perfect place to make the call. Everyone was posed to listen as he made the biggest decision of his young life. Those listening also included impressionable young athletes from our little town who looked to him for leadership and guidance. They were so excited. He went into a room with his dad to visit one last time about his decision. We had all prayed together before, and now we waited. But when they exited that room, I could see it on Tillman's face. Tears were streaming down, and he announced to all of those gathered that he was not yet sensing God's peace in this decision. The air left the room, and I confess I thought he was going to lose the opportunity. We left and went home. It was around 8 p.m.

At 8:30 p.m., the phone rang.

"Son, this is Coach Tim Brewster from The University of Texas Football program."

Tillman said those words suddenly sent a power surge from his head to toes, and he listened intently as Coach Brewster asked if he could come see Tillman play in Denver. Of course Tillman, aware of all the family history with the University of Texas, told Brewster he looked forward to meeting him. In the next week, two coaches arrived at Tillman's little 2A high school athletic department and stayed to watch the team's practice. They offered Tillman a full-ride to Texas. He said the peace of God swelled over him like nothing before and the whisper he had waited for was finally a yell in his spiritual ear. He accepted and started his four-year stint as a Longhorn.

I knew somehow this entire football scholarship to Texas scenario had been orchestrated by God and when it came down to it, was not really about football. I realized God was doing something through this situation that met a deep longing I had to know my father. When we are waiting for God to speak to us, we must realize He is doing things at so many different levels. Had Tillman gone to Nebraska, which was his dream, and had he not waited for that still, small voice, there would not have been the beginning of a long and overdue healing between my father and me.

I am not presumptuous enough to think this was the only reason for Tillman's acceptance to Texas, but at my level of the equation, it created an open door between my father and me that had not been opened ever before. I could count on one hand the times I had spent with my dad since he left. I had adored him and so had my mother, and now, in the most unusual way, I felt I might have a small chance at knowing him, not as the myth, but as my dad and as a grandfather.

No one from Basalt, Colorado, went to Texas on a full-ride football scholarship from a 2A little Christian school. It was possibly an answer to years of prayer, and as I received many calls from my father about Tillman's career at Texas, I realized that I was talking to him more than I ever had in my lifetime. The grief of losing my father had been with me all of my life, just below the surface of the tears right behind my eyes. But God had a plan from the beginning to suture my heart together with my dad.

Much later and as I stood there holding my father's hand when he was dying, his rough, huge hands like mine, the hands I had always remembered, the touch of the generations was pulsing through my veins. I knew without a doubt I was there in that moment because one young man had heard and leaned into the whispers of the heart of God.

For the Love

When my children were very young, long before the opportunity for my son to go to the same university in Texas where my father had also been the All-American, God dealt with my hurt related to my father in a most gentle and precious manner.

My husband and I were very involved with a large Montessori school, and as he became the Chairman of the Board of that school, we decided it best to move the school to a new and more prominent location. The new school building was to be built on the same site as the Episcopal school, sharing common ground and some facilities. It was a brilliant move and soon made our little school one of the most sought after schools in the area. But with that move came a decision to let the headmaster go, and replace her with a more competent and sympathetic head. I say, "sympathetic," because we were having difficulties from staff and some parents who did not like the fact that the school would in any way be associated with the Episcopal school.

At one time, there were even threats that tomatoes might be thrown at my husband in PTA meetings and that those in opposition to the move did not like any affiliation with Christianity at all. Simultaneously, while installing this new head of the school, my husband approached the board asking their permission to install a cornerstone on the new and beautiful building. On that cornerstone, he wanted this to be chiseled in the stone:

> *"Let your light so shine before men, that they may see your good works and glorify your Father in heaven."* Matthew 5:16

An uproar from some faculty and these same disgruntled parents became unmanageable for the new headmistress. She called Don and asked if the cornerstone could be removed to make peace. This scripture flashed through his mind. "They take not my life from Me, but I lay it down, (John 10:18)" and with that Don gave her permission to remove the stone.

In the midst of the chaos, I was also personally going through a trial of my own. Everywhere I went, every message I heard, every sermon I listened to, and everything I read had the same thread of a message - Love of the Father ... You know love, like Abba, Daddy.

But the truth was, I knew little of that kind of love and questioned my heavenly Father about it. If love from God was anything like the love of my earthly father, it meant:

I am leaving and never coming back.
I never call or check in with you.
I haven't seen you grow up, become a young woman.
I live forty minutes away and yet in fifteen years, I have seen you twice.

I trusted God in many ways and as it is with many things in the healing process, I could not make the transitional jump in my heart from "daddy's love" to the love of Abba, Father. I think at some level I must have been afraid that if I trusted God as my father, He could only let me down; a deadbeat, like my father turned out to be. But still there was something so deep in my heart that knew my father had loved me and still did love me.

As I was in church (don't forget the school story that is simultaneously unfolding) one morning, and the sermon was, you guessed it, "The Love of the Father -Daddy Love." The pastor asked a strange but haunting question at the end of his talk. He asked, "Look around you and tell me, who in this room does God not love as a father?" In my mind's eye, I thought of all the people I knew in this fellowship and slowly looked around the room. I felt there was not one person in that room that God did not love as a father, not one. Until my heart's gaze fell upon me, I could not believe God really loved me as a father, true and faithful. I could not even go there in my mind until my heart broke in two, right there in church.

I began to weep and grieve like someone who had just witnessed a most beloved friend die in front of them. As I sobbed through my heartache, the grief so real that I could barely take a breath, I heard the pastor call forward anyone who needed to go for prayer. Certainly he meant me, so I stood up, tears hot on my face, running down my chin, and falling onto the floor. I cried all the way to the basement altar where I knelt down.

Just as I knelt down, an elder beckoned me over to stand before him. He looked just like you might imagine your father or grandfather might look. His eyes were kind and gentle, his hands, large and authoritative. He took my wet face into those hands and prayed words I never really heard; but I did hear this, "You are mine. I love you, child of mine." And as that man took his bare hands and wiped the snot that was dripping off the end of my nose and the hot tears and smeared mascara off my face, I heard my Heavenly Father say, "I love you like this."

Gentle. Shouldering. Unashamed. Deep. Holding. Soft. Quiet. Strong.

My heart was melting into a love that I had never experienced before, Abba, Father Love.

At school the next morning, I drove my children through the carpool drop-off line, passing right by the cornerstone that had been removed. They had chosen to remove the words by cementing in the chiseled words on the stone. So with a trowel they had filled in the words and had taken broad smearing strokes all over the side of that building. As my eyes met this image, all I could hear was, "I loved you this much…That they took my words and smeared them all over this building…That they took my body and broke it…That they took my side and pierced it for you. Just for you. Child of Mine."

I drove around for three hours weeping and absorbing this love that my heart had longed for ever since my own father had left. It was tangible. Real. Deep. Complete. The next day, I drove through the carpool line and there on the side of that building (wet tears are flowing even now as I am writing), where they had smeared those words hoping to fill them in, the cornerstone had been sanded to clean up the surface. They had failed at true coverage since the mortar they used was a lighter color than the background of the stone and the words shone forth from the inside out even brighter and more legible than before.

> *"Let your light so shine before men, that they may see your **good works** and glorify your Father in heaven."* Matthew 5:16

God spoke to me, calling me to truly understand the love of a father, and in doing so, opened the door of my broken heart so I might be healed. It was that healing that years later opened the door to the relationship I was able to have with my father before he died. There are times the Lord speaks to us by opening doors. Our responsibility is to trust Him and the reasons He has for opening the doors.

Luke 8

... But as he went the people thronged him.

> *"And a woman having an issue of blood twelve years, which had spent all her living upon physicians, neither could be healed of any."* Luke 8:43

Jesus was pressed in on every side. On every side, desperate people wanted His word, His touch, and His healing presence. Remember, He was on His way to answer the call of Jairus as He had been called to save Jairus' daughter's life. As Jesus sees only what the Father in heaven is doing, He stops to take His time with a woman who had been on her menstrual period for twelve long years, obviously in great need of a physician. This desperate and culturally "unclean" woman had been ostracized and cast out of any normal life that her sickness precluded her from attaining. She was poor, both in finances and in spirit. She had spent her life looking for a relief, and discouraged and weak, she took the moment to reach for a possible cure. She already had enough faith to reach out to Him. It took tremendous faith because she, in her relentless condition was considered "unclean" by societal norm. She was risking stoning for breaking the law that stated she must not come into crowds or touch anyone during her time of blood. The anguish she must have known to risk being seen and to touch a man in her condition is shown by her bold and courageous search for healing.

In her faith, she,

> *"Came behind him, and touched the border of his garment: and immediately her issue of blood stanched."* Luke 8:44

I often ask, "Why?" when in scripture I see little added words or facts that seem irrelevant to the themes expressed. I think no word is wasted and in God's great economy, there is meaning in every word. "Border (hem) of His garment..." Why was it so important for God to tell us that she touched Jesus there? His garment was woven like many Rabbis from flax, overlaid with a cloak while under it lay a "tzi-tzi" or prayer shawl with fringe. Imagine Him pressed on every side, crowded and as He walked, and out from under His cloak swung the knotted tassels of His tzi-tzi fringe. He would have knotted those strings to hang down below his garment and to be an ever-present reminder of the names of God. Names that in all situations could be reached for and called upon. She braved the crowd and, not even needing to see His face, reached up to touch the hem of that garment that was laden with the names of God. One such specific name would have been, "Jehovah – Rapha." God my healer. With humility, she faced God in her deepest pain and loss. She had probably been ostracized from all family, husband, friends, and children, and in her direst moment, she reached for the One who would never turn her away. At risk of life and limb, she knew, by faith, He would heal her.

> *"And Jesus said, Who touched me? When all denied, Peter and they that were with him said, Master, the multitude throng thee and press thee, and sayest thou, Who touched me?"* Luke 8:45

It might have been impossible for any man to know who had touched him as the throngs of people crushed in and hundreds of hands brushed into his sides. But Jesus knew someone had touched Him with a heartfelt and serious need. He didn't realize this by the physical pressure on His leg. He didn't know this because He could feel the heat of her hand. He didn't sense he touch because he saw it with His eyes or felt it in His nervous system.

> *"And Jesus said, Somebody hath touched me: for I perceive that virtue is gone out of me."* Luke 8:46

He felt power leave Him. He, by the might of His spiritual presence, felt power leave Him to transfer healing to her. Virtue is defined here as "supply of faith" and "intrinsic eminence" or "moral goodness." A supply of faith and goodness and eminence left Jesus and transferred to her. As we know that "faith is a gift from God" (Ephesians 2:8), we also realize that later in this passage when Jesus tells her "her faith has made her well," that same faith was a gift from Him. She first "believed only." She stepped out into the risk, into the unknown by faith. Jesus met her there with even more faith and she was healed.

"And when the woman saw that she was not hid, she came trembling, and falling down before him, she declared unto him before all the people for what cause she had touched him, and how she was healed immediately. And he said unto her, Daughter, be of good comfort: thy faith hath made thee whole; go in peace." Luke 8:47-48

CHAPTER SEVEN:
LISTEN BEHIND
Learning to Hear and See as God Does

Learning to listen behind is a critical component of learning to hear and obey the whispers of God. It opens the eyes of our heart to the pain we see in others. It allows us to see them the way God sees them and to hear what their hearts are actually saying.

God used my childhood to show me people's hurts and broken hearts. He opened the eyes of my heart to the pain in theirs, and He taught me to listen behind what was being said. And trust me, it can be scary being knee-deep in people's unspoken needs. Pointing them out and opening them up can be tricky and frightening as well. But hearts can be healed when opened to love, acceptance, and truth. Freedom can come when trust, and compassion allows someone to feel truly known. When we are known by someone, truly known, and there is acceptance and love, without judgment or comparison, it acts as a soothing oil that seeps into every crevice of a broken and damaged heart.

Rescue

Rescuing my mother was something I learned quickly would never be easy. She was always quick to spew out all sorts of character maligning and slanderous accusations toward Don and me when we were trying to get her to hospitals and treatment centers. She had begun to lock herself in her dark room, never coming out for weeks at a time. She had her meals prepared for her under strict orders to be left outside her door, and she frequently made delivery calls to the local liquor store. She was stealing prescription pads from doctors and befriending every pharmacist in the area, giving them tickets to professional ball games and gifts of money, all to keep her medications stocked. We found multiple boxes of empty pill bottles stashed in her closets and alcohol bottles hidden in shopping bags. In fact, her pills and her alcohol were stashed in every drawer, every closet, every handbag, in boots, and trash bags all over her house. She could look me right in the face, drink in hand, and tell me she was not drinking.

The former beauty queen had turned on us all. Heartsick from an empty life, my mother had escaped for one of the last times from a locked facility and invited some motorcycle gang members she had met there to her house so they could rummage through her silver, fine china, jewelry, and furs, only to rob her blind. One night she had been found wandering the streets of the most exclusive neighborhood where she lived, confused after she had almost taken the side off her garage when she backed out of the driveway. She had turned from this beautiful and loving woman into a shadow of her body, mind, and spirit.

It absolutely and completely broke my heart. I was searching to find an answer. I cried many tears for many years. I was lonely in the search, and I was confused with her choices. I asked myself, "Why was her love for my sister and me not enough for her to stop?" For years I believed the lie that I was simply not enough. The only thing left to do was to cry out to God.

At one stage of my mother's deep-sinking alcoholism, I began practicing something I called "strengthening myself in the Lord." I believed God gave me this to help me cope with the trauma of her drinking. Each time I encountered her in her bizarre and hurtful behavior, I strengthened myself in the Lord. I listened to awesome worship music and I prayed, asking for wisdom and direction, sometimes asking God to give me the exact words He would have me say, even in the moment I was saying them. If I felt myself sinking amidst one of her terrible storms, I looked to Him quickly, and it was as if I had been given all the strength I needed to face the next horrible episode with her.

One day we received a call from the hospital that our 50-year-old, beautiful, Elizabeth Taylor-looking, blue eyed mother was dying in intensive care. We were all summoned to come as quickly as possible. Her intake of one large and full bottle of Valium along with two bottles of vodka had passed her out on the floor of a posh hotel room. With doors locked and the "Do Not Disturb" sign keeping anyone from seeing her deadly act, she curled up on the floor and waited to die. She had aspirated her own vomit and lay on the cold tile floor. Had it not been for the housekeeper, who after three days called management, mother would have died in that room on that cold and unforgiving floor. Rushed by ambulance, she was now in intensive care fighting for her life. Respirator, monitors, and catheters could not keep up with the edge of vital suppression she was up against. She had suppressed all of her breathing, heart rhythm, bone marrow, and liver and kidney functions to the point that we all waited beside her bed, ready to say goodbye.

I prayed. I cried. I prayed. I cried out to God, "Save. Her. Please. Save. Her," and He did.

She was alive; hope was alive. My precious husband always told me when faced with yet another call for her rescue, "Where there is life, honey, there is hope. We hope that she can be saved."

Hope. Hope. Hope. Did I ever cling to that hope. I would be on my way to doctor's meetings, lawyer meetings, and "guardian-of-her–person" meetings, and all I knew to do was to cry out to God. He was so real I could feel His physical presence in the room with me during those meetings. I found myself saying things to the lawyers and judges that only He would have said for me. I had no other strength but His to take care of the situation. I could hear His whispers of power and hope.

My father had acquiesced his responsibility and left it up to my husband and me. I was young, married with four of my five children; the fifth came along in the middle of some of her last treatments. I was working hard at recognizing and listening to that still, calming, and strong voice in my heart. I knew it was God guiding me, and I tried to obey every word I interpreted as Him. I leaned into it. I sought peace in the waves and calm in the middle of the raging storm for family, my marriage, and myself. I wanted to keep my grief from spilling into them. I so desperately wanted "different" for all of them. The hurt lay right behind my eyes. It took little for it to come spilling out at any mention of my mother's condition.

See Her As I Do

Life went on. She got worse. I heard more and more clearly from Jesus. He was clearing out my heart, calling me to trust and know Him regardless of my mother's outcome. He was reaching into the most inner part of my heart and teaching me His ways. As I mentioned before, His presence was so real to me that at times I felt I could physically reach out and touch him.

One day I heard His still voice saying, "Do you trust Me with your mom? Why are you wearing that badge of pain as your identity? Can you let Me be your badge of identity? Can you let Me be the One you identify yourself with in place of your pain and all your plans to fix it? Can you **believe,** no matter the outcome with your mom, that I am *most* interested in your heart being all in with me? I want you, dear child of mine. I want all of your heart. I want you to know that I am God and you are not. You are not in control, nor do you have to try to be any longer."

He went on to say, "I want you to see your mom with My eyes. I see her whole, healed and well. I love her more than you ever can. When you look at her, when she speaks those accusations and obscenities to you, I want you to remember that she is not that bottle of pills you see. She is not that bottle of alcohol that speaks through her. I am going to give you eyes to see her as I do. Listen behind her pain. See her as I do."

"LISTEN BEHIND HER PAIN AND SEE HER AS I DO."
"I will give you eyes to see her and ears to hear her like I do."

The last time I saw her was right before Valentine's Day. She was in very bad shape and could hardly recognize me most of the two days I was there. She was only sixty-four. She was holed up in her room, lying on her bed. I knelt down by her bed and stroked her hair, her forehead. She slowly opened her eyes and spoke to me. As I steeled myself for what she might say, all I heard at that moment was the voice of the Lord saying, "She's mine. Listen behind her pain. See her the way I see her. Don't be afraid. Don't be angry anymore."

She then spoke this to me. "I am so sorry, my Angel Paige." She had called me Angel Paige all of my life. "I cannot stop. I cannot quit this thing. It is more than me. I love you, and I am so sorry. So, so sorry."

It was the only time she had admitted any remorse to me. As I closed the door behind me and looked at her, I did not know it was the last time I would ever see her. We found her two months later having died after getting up in the middle of the night, presumably for more to drink or more pills to take. She collapsed on the side of her bed, alone in her room. We flew in from Colorado to plan and be there for her funeral. My husband. Me. My five children. And God. We were all there.

Whole and Healed

Now, I consider myself to be a fairly capable person, and know I can handle things well in a crisis. The funeral home called and asked me to pick out a burial outfit for my mom. In all my capable-ness, I stood there gazing into her closet that was filled with her clothes. It took me three hours to just stand there and hold her things close to my heart. I smelled the perfume on her dresses and blouses. I could not, for the life of me, give over those clothes for this one last time. I was frozen in this moment of letting go, as I grieved, listened, and remembered. I loved her so.

With tears streaming down my face, I closed my eyes, praying to God and holding the suit, blouse, and jewelry we would bury her in. It was so very surreal. As I was leaving her house for one of the last times before her funeral, with eyes closed, I stood in the room she died in. In that moment, I saw an image. It was in my heart's eye - a vision if you want to call it that. There was this figure of a man, standing too close to me for me to distinguish who it was. As this figure in the vision walked further and further away, I began to distinguish the form of what was a picture of Him. His back was toward me. I knew in my heart it was Jesus. He was carrying something . . . someone. He held a woman whose legs were draped across His outstretched arms. I could see an arm wrapped around His shoulders and her head rested against His chest, as if a sleeping child that was resting in her father's arms. His shoulders somehow seemed to bear the whole weight of this moment, the grief, the sin, everything. As I looked, and just as He was almost from sight, my mother's head dropped back over His arm and she looked back and right into my eyes. Her face was young, vibrant, and alive. Her smile was aglow; deep, safe, rich and at peace with joy indescribable. Her eyes were full with that joy and were steel blue, piercing my heart. Her smile seemed to pour out from the corners of her eyes. She squinted as if to say, "I'm safe now, I'm healed now, and I'm whole now, my Angel Paige." Even now as I write this, I can see her face, whole, healed, and well.

Just as He had seen her all along,
He had promised to give me eyes to see her as He did.

Today as I write this, my heart literally aches and my tears still swell. My throat is tight. I wish I were a painter, and I could paint what I saw in my heart that day. I know it was a gift from God as He was whispering once again to my heart. "I gave you eyes to see her the way I see her. Try to see everyone you can with those same eyes. Learn to hear everyone's heart the way I heard hers, and the way I hear yours. Learn to listen behind what you see."

Jesus said, "I have come that they may have life, and have it more abundantly." – John 10:10

Life in this world is not without pain and suffering. He has promised us "trial and tribulation" but He has also promised us an abundant life. Abundant life is living in the tension of the pain yet still resting in Him. Abiding in Jesus and resting in the Lord of the Sabbath.

He said, "My yoke is easy and My burden is light. Therefore, pick up your cross and follow Me." – Matthew 11:30

Never Thirst Again

> *"So He came to a city of Samaria, which is called Sychar, near the plot of ground that Jacob gave to his son Joseph. Now Jacob's well was there. Jesus therefore, being wearied from His journey, sat thus by the well. It was about the sixth hour."*
> John 4: 5-6

Make a note that Jesus and the people of Israel were at odds with the people in Samaria. Samaritans had developed their own compromised form of the practice of Judaism. The Samaritans still believed in the Jewish God of Abraham, Isaac, and Jacob, but they worshiped on Mount Gerizim (instead of Jerusalem) with their own worship traditions. The Samaritans also had their own Books of the Law, not the Pentateuch from Moses, and it was written in Aramaic. Samaritans also did not, and to this day, do not accept the poetic and prophetic books of the Hebrew Scriptures. The Samaritans built a temple on Mount Gerizim in around 400 B.C. Because of this, there was a lot of tension and hostility between the Jews and the Samaritans. This was the climate of the relationship between these two groups as Jesus, the Jewish rabbi, approached the Samaritan woman at the well.

> *"A woman of Samaria came to draw water. Jesus said to her, "Give Me a drink." For His disciples had gone away into the city to buy food."* John 4:7-8

I am wondering if God didn't include this sentence to show us that the disciples might never have wanted to be seen passing through the Samaritan woman's territory. It is likely God shows us this so that we can see His attention to the details of His plan. We must never forget that He is in the details of our lives. He calls us to see the unlovely; to hear His words of truth and love for them.

> *"Then the woman of Samaria said to Him, "How is it that You, being a Jew, ask a drink from me, a Samaritan woman?" For Jews have no dealings with Samaritans. Jesus answered and said to her, "If you knew the gift of God, and whom it is who says to you, 'Give Me a drink,' you would have asked Him, and He would have given you living water."* John 4:9-10

Jesus, like other stories of Moses and Abraham, identifies Himself with the power of God. He promises here to bring life and deliverance for all those in need.

> *"The woman said to Him, "Sir, You have nothing to draw with, and the well is deep. Where then do You get that living water? Are You greater than our father Jacob, who gave us the well, and drank from it himself, as well as his sons and his livestock?" Jesus answered and said to her, "Whoever drinks of this water will thirst again, but whoever drinks of the water that I shall give him will never thirst. But the water that I shall give him will become in him a fountain of water springing up into everlasting life."* John 4: 11-14

Jesus is talking to her here about a spiritual "water," one that fills and saves. He is speaking of Himself. He is promising an everlasting life in Him. It would be difficult for her to receive this news from Him, a Jew; but she listens. He continues to open her heart to the knowledge of Him as her Savior, no matter her preconceived notion of the Jews and their long-awaited Messiah.

> *"The woman said to Him, "Sir, give me this water, that I may not thirst, nor come here to draw." Jesus said to her, "Go, call your husband, and come here."* John 4:15-16

I make note it is here that Jesus is reaching deep into her heart. He, having all knowledge, fully God, and fully man, knows the deceits and motives of the heart. It is important as we study the Bible, to ask ourselves questions when we see God place something in a narrative that seemingly has no continuity with the story. He has suddenly changed the direction of the dialogue to include her husband. We must then ask, "Why?" We will find answers there we never knew in the whispers of a truth, hidden in the story. It is there we can hear with our spiritual ears and develop an understanding of Him that is far deeper than if we were only taking it at the surface meaning. This is another way we discern the whispers of our Savior.

> *"The woman answered and said, "I have no husband." Jesus said to her, "You have well said, 'I have no husband,' for you have had five husbands, and the one whom you now have is not your husband; in that you spoke truly."* John 4: 17-18

Whoa! What an unveiling Jesus has done upon this meeting of His heart with hers. He has cut through the superficial greetings and has pricked her heart with the knowledge He shares in the middle of her sad, but deceptive story. She has implied, not knowing that Jesus is in fact omniscient God, that she only has one husband when she really has known five. In this convicting statement by Jesus, had it not been true, or if He were not delivering it in some unfathomable and extremely loving way, the woman at the well is taken to her knees by the honest and confronting truth of her situation. She must be, in some way, overwhelmed by the love of a Savior who has opened her heart, seen it, revealed the ugliness in it, healed it, and then lovingly, as He always does, put it back together.

> *"The woman said to Him, "Sir, I perceive that You are a prophet. Our fathers worshiped on this mountain, and you Jews say that in Jerusalem is the place where one ought to worship." Jesus said to her, "Woman, believe Me, the hour is coming when you will neither on this mountain, nor in Jerusalem, worship the Father. You worship what you do not know; we know what we worship, for salvation is of the Jews. But the hour is coming, and now is, when the true worshipers will worship the Father in spirit and truth; for the Father is seeking such to worship Him. God is Spirit, and those who worship Him must worship in spirit and truth."* Luke 4:19-24

He declares, once again, to her that His power is from on high. He declares Himself imbued with a power that comes from the Spirit of God. He announces no matter what the differences have been between the Samaritan and Jew, one must personally decide who Messiah is to them. He leads her to a knowledge that overrides experience and transcends earthly form. He leads her to eternal decisions that are for her salvation and for everlasting life. He must have said all these things with such love, such conviction, that the Holy Spirit dwelling and overshadowing Him, emanated from Him to absorb her every pore, penetrate her every fiber.

> *"The woman said to Him, "I know that Messiah is coming" (who is called Christ). "When He comes, He will tell us all things." Jesus said to her, "I who speak to you am He."* Once again, Jesus declares

> the great "I AM." And at this point His disciples came, and they marveled that He talked with a woman; yet no one said, "What do You seek?" or, "Why are You talking with her?" Luke 4:25-27

After what must now be a scene that has a "foreign" woman at the very knees of Jesus, and one that did not include any arguing or backlash, the disciples must sense the presence of God though the power of the Holy Spirit as they say nothing to Jesus about being with her.

> "The woman then left her water pot, went her way into the city, and said to the men, "Come, see a Man who told me all things that I ever did. Could this be the Christ?" Then they went out of the city and came to Him. Luke 4:28-30

Her worship response to Jesus the Messiah was to go into her city and declare Him the Savior of the world. She had the common response of one who had been bound by sin and was suddenly and unexpectedly set free from the life once lived apart from God. She has a similar response as the blind man who is given his sight, or Jairus when his daughter was healed, or Mary when told she was to be the mother of Jesus, or Hannah when she was required to give her son to the service of God. Her response is ours when confronted with the new life and living water that Jesus offers. When we hear His whisper in our ear, "Come follow Me and I will give you water that you would never thirst again, that your life would be full and that you would have life abundant."

> "And many of the Samaritans of that city believed in Him because of the word of the woman who testified, "He told me all that I ever did." So

when the Samaritans had come to Him, they urged Him to stay with them; and He stayed there two days. And many more believed because of His own word. Then they said to the woman, "Now we believe, not because of what you said, for we ourselves have heard Him and we know that this is indeed the Christ, [a] the Savior of the world."
Luke 4: 39-42

How often have we encountered our own woman at the well and been unsure how to see her, listen to her, and make her feel known and loved? Just as Jesus interacted with the woman at the well and just as he loved my mother, He loves you and me and wants the same thing for us. He wants us never to thirst again. It is why I know that God desires for each of us to hear His voice. Because to experience the living water that Jesus offers, we must be able to hear His voice. We must not put our trust nor have our faith in any predetermined outcome. We must place our hope in Him alone. Though my mother's story did not end as I had prayed; I learned that God is God and I'm not. The purposes rendered through the loss of my mother are used for good, as promised. They have worked compassion and love, patience and long-suffering where it was not fully developed before. It is in His identity alone that I receive mine.

CONCLUSION

The first study I ever did in the Old Testament was on the Tabernacle. The Tabernacle was the God-inspired place of worship for the nation of Israel who found themselves wandering in the desert on their way to the long awaited, "Promised Land." We reviewed its design in detail by wading through the instructions laid out by God to Moses in Exodus 26. I painstakingly dissected the scripture as it referenced the materials and exact dimensions. He ordered that Moses construct a "mobile" sanctuary for the worshipful practice of the Jews while they wandered in the desert wilderness.

Isn't it so like God to give us a plan for "seeing" Him even when we willfully wander and stray from His presence? Isn't it so like Him to give us a way to be near even when we don't readily see Him?

"Moreover you shall make the Tabernacle *with* ten curtains *of* fine woven linen and blue, purple, and scarlet *thread;* with artistic designs of cherubim you shall weave them. The length of each curtain *shall be* twenty-eight cubits, and the width of each curtain four cubits. And every one of the curtains shall have the same measurements. Five curtains shall be coupled to one another, and *the other* five curtains *shall be* coupled to one another. ... Exodus 26:1-6

Every part of the details of this design whispers the presence of God and hints at the foreshadowing of Christ to come. Every part of God's place of worship was a picture of Christ, His kingdom rhythm and the glory of His God/Man/King/Priest/Savior status from the beginning of time. The timeless revelation is illustrated in the Tabernacle and transcends from past kingdom (Jewish nation wandering in the desert for forty years), to present kingdom (from the birth of Christ until now), and then to future kingdom (Christ will come again). If we, as readers of this depiction, look at only the physical description, we miss the whisper of God that quietly, yet powerfully, calls us to hear,

"Are you quiet enough to see my Son in this tabernacle design, the systems of sacrifice and glory, the veiled access to the throne, and mercy triumphing over law? Can you understand that even seven hundred years before Christ was born, I showed Him to you in the tabernacle architecture? Can you hear me whisper to your heart that I am near? Are you prepared to see that "I Am" there, here, and coming again? Can you listen to my whisper as I am showing you more deeply who I am and that I have always been? Could it be that in the busy-ness of your life, you are missing me still? Missing ME as they did?"

Scripture is the revelation of Jesus Christ, especially full of prophesies in the Old Testament. It is there He whispers in the account in Genesis where He says, "Let Us make man in Our image." (Genesis 1:26) This use of the plural Elohim (Us and Our) to mean God from the beginning of creation displays the relationship in the Trinity. I can hear God whisper, "I am." In the history of Noah, Abraham and Isaac, and Joseph with his coat of many colors, one can discern God's message hidden in the lines of His Word. Noah's Ark and its construction of tar-covered acacia wood are a picture of the cross and the Christ who carries us into salvation, who baptizes us with new hope and freedom from sin, down into the water and raised again in new life. The sacrifice Abraham makes as he raises his dagger to slay his only begotten son as Isaac is tied to the altar, a lamb is in the thicket and is revealed and sacrificed in his stead. Even Joseph, youngest son of Jacob, was betrayed by his brothers and left to die an excruciating death. Joseph was raised from the pit and went to become the ruler over all, the king's right hand man, a son of sorts. In these foreshadows of Jesus, I can see the vastness of God in scripture. I can hear His voice call to me to know Him more clearly, love Him more dearly, and learn His ways of Kingdom listening ... His whispers.

Dance

Do not be fooled into thinking God is some slot machine where we get to speak what we want, pull the lever, and hit the jackpot, and then go about our merry way. Rather, He is the quiet and soft-spoken Shepherd who leads us in paths of righteousness (right standing with Him) to glorify His name. His voice can lead us quietly, or it may press on our hearts fiercely, and in that way His whispers seem loud.

Tim Keller writes in his book, *Jesus the King*, that God the Father, the Son, and the Holy Spirit, from the beginning of time have been in a "dance" together. The path of Sh'ma, hearing and obeying, is the great way we get to learn the *dance*, the communion with our heavenly Father. They are one together and have invited us into the joy of their relationship. As we enter into relationship with them, we are entreated to the joy of being one with them as they are one together. He calls us to this great and twirling romance, an invitation that only proves how much He intimately loves us. It is an unfathomable gift to fall into the love of the living God. He wants that "dance" to be all we need to fulfill us and meet our every need.

He never leaves us once we begin the dance. He leads us because He has great adventures and gifts for us, and most importantly, because He wants us to know Him and love Him, and to dance with only Him. I have known and do know the incredible depths of the love of God. But I couldn't possibly know the depths of His love for me had I not known the darkness of the losses I have endured and the emptiness of my time without Him. God's great contrast is that in order for me to hear and know Him, I must know what is there in contrast to that great love. I cannot truly know "light" unless I have experienced "darkness." This is where I learn gratefulness for the pain.

God Is Not In That Box We Put Him In

Perhaps one of the greatest times of learning to see the light through the darkness came when my nephew, Russell, was born. My sister-in-law was due in just a few short months, and she and the whole family were anticipating their firstborn. She was in San Marcos, Texas, outside of Austin, when we got the call. My brother-in-law phoned us and said, "Come quickly, Sherri is in labor!" My head went a little tilt with excitement until I remembered the reality that she was not due for over three more months. "What did you say?" I replied now with angst in my voice. He confirmed that she was indeed in labor and yes the baby, if it were at all possible would be born only after six and a half months of being in the womb.

We rushed, we prayed, we whirl-winded out of Houston to meet my brother-in law-in Austin, about a three hour drive from Houston. My husband went straight there from his office while I gathered all my four chicks from school and naps. We were packed up and on our way.

When we arrived at the hospital, the baby had been born at under two pounds and was hooked to every machine imaginable; every orifice of his little body filled with a tube. His skin was almost translucent; eyes closed, as his vital signs were monitored by a full team of experts. It turned out that Seton Hospital is one of the foremost hospitals for premature infants. They had a window to the NICU so that family could view the baby's progress. We stood there in awe and fear as our prayers began the moment we saw the plaque in the hall, which read, "<u>We treat every patient as Christ Himself.</u>" We found comfort and peace as we paced the floors on his behalf. It was touch and go all day but he was fighting for his little life. There was no sign of my sister-

CONCLUSION

in-law as she would go in to see him by herself, filled with grief and horror at what could be.

We stayed there together all day, watching and waiting. He was battling hard, every breath a miracle, every beat of his heart counted as progress. We left in the night to take our four children to sleep in a nearby hotel. We kept our ears to the phone, expecting a worst-case scenario call any minute. Finally, we were able to sleep after our many prayers were given over to God.

At 3 AM., the phone rang, and it was my brother-in-law. He told Don that his baby was in distress, and we needed to come over immediately. As we wiped sleep from our and our children's weary eyes and we were working at getting everyone dressed, Don said he had had a dream and did not sleep well. I answered with a quick, "me too" but made him tell me first. He told me he had been restless all night, and that the Lord was speaking to him about the baby, Russell. He felt as if God were telling him over and over again to baptize the baby. When he said that, I told him I, too, was awakened by whispers I believed to be God that also said to baptize the baby. We both did not even understand that direction but confirmed it must be God since we both had heard the same thing. Since we both believed baptism had to be full immersion, an action based on the baptizee's choice to follow Jesus, we weren't sure why God would want us to baptize an infant. But we also knew that God was speaking to us both in the exact same way and at the exact same time. So we willingly submitted to God, recognizing that He is able to do it any way he pleased. He often will shake up the box we place Him in to teach us not to put Him in there in the first place. His wisdom can be confounding and show us how He loves without rules and teaches by making us aware of the vastness of His ways.

So our mission going in was to baptize that baby even though it confounded earthly, even biblical wisdom as we knew it.

When we arrived early that morning, the observation hall was shut off to any visitors. In an instant, Don and I knew this was probably because our baby Russell was in deep distress, and the hospital staff was probably doing all they could to save his little life. We waited, prayed, and paced for over two hours. With sleepy children sprawled out in the hospital waiting room and my brother-in-law giving us updates, the situation was dire. Little Russell's life was on the edge; his lungs had collapsed, and his oxygen saturation was low. His heart was racing to keep him alive, and he was quickly tiring of the battle. We were finally shown to the hall and were able to see his tiny body racked with straining for life and tubes now piercing his little side.

We prayed. We prayed for Jesus to heal and to save. We told his dad and his mom that God had told us to baptize the baby and that we, as believers, could come in and in the name of Jesus, baptize that child. Obedience to God's call seems sometimes to be a foolish act that the Holy Spirit keeps prodding and prompting us to do. The oxygen saturation digital read was now at 39 percent. It is supposed to stay near 99 to 100 percent. We prayed. We baptized that little boy and although the doctors told us that survival would bring all kinds of learning issues; perhaps blindness; deafness, or mental retardation; we "believed only" God.

Once he was baptized, the burden we felt to do so lifted. One hour after his miniature head and hands were dipped in the water; the digital read out in red looked something like this: 39; 40; 45; 55; 62; 70; 72; 80; 88; 90; 93; and by the long awaited hours of mid-morning, Russell was stabilized and his oxygen saturation was 99 percent. That boy survived and now is a young man who knows the power of God as we were blessed to tell him that miraculous story of his start in life. He suffered none of the things the doctors were afraid of, and we can all only give glory to God. He speaks and we somehow, through the fog and fear, can hear him. We had prayed for years for his mother and father to know Jesus. When asked about the turning point for their son's survival, they both agreed it was when he was baptized. I know this: that God works in mysterious ways to draw those whom He loves to Himself.

Sometimes, we must experience the dark to see the light and the glory of God. He gives us these moments, not to cause us pain, but to build our faith, and to reveal Himself to us in ways our "box" would never allow us to see Him.

Come Forth

> *"Upon his arrival, Jesus found that Lazarus had already been in the tomb for four days. 18 Now Bethany was less than two miles from Jerusalem, 19 and many Jews had come to Martha and Mary to comfort them in the loss of their brother. 20 When Martha heard that Jesus was coming, she went out to meet him, but Mary stayed at home."*
> - John 11:17-20

Lazarus, their brother, was dead. Mary and Martha were beyond themselves, unable to understand what had caused Jesus to tarry, overcome with grief at the loss of their beloved brother. Such darkness and despair. Even in the midst of those who were there to comfort them, they could not be comforted. And then word arrived that Jesus had finally come. Perhaps again we see the picture of Martha-the-doer and Mary-the-contemplative. Martha running to meet Jesus shows us the reality of her faith in Him as if to say, "He's here; now all will be right." Mary, meanwhile, may know that in her solitude, her faith is strengthened. Hope was becoming dim and distant…until Jesus. When He arrived, I pictured all clamoring around and scurrying with great expectancy. The energy immediately shifted from despair to hope.

> *21 "Lord," Martha said to Jesus, "if you had been here, my brother would not have died. 22 But I know that even now God will give you whatever you ask." –* John 11:21-22

Martha then openly declares her fear of regret in missed opportunity in Jesus' absence; and then announces her incredible faith that even in the middle of it, all will be rectified-because He is now here!

> *23 "Jesus said to her, "Your brother will rise again." Jesus immediately meets and answers her faith with His beautiful response. 24 Martha answered, "I know he will rise again in the resurrection at the last day."* John 11:23-24

Martha's statement proves her disbelief that even her faith could be applicable to her situation personally. She switches strangely to lofty ideas of resurrection, clarifying to all around and declaring even to Jesus, that resurrection couldn't possibly be personal for right here and right now. How often do I spiritualize my faith to the point of being "no earthly good" for the here and now? How often is it a way to speak of ideals in faith instead of applying them practically and personally? I understand Martha, how crazy it feels to think that Jesus came just for you and that He might just have that miracle you think is so far out of your reach. I have been that girl who thinks the answer comes in a certain lofty theological and religious concept when faith is present in the details of the here and now. If I would only believe, only trust Him at His word. Could it actually be possible? For even me?

> *25 "Jesus said to her, "I am the resurrection and the life. The one who believes in me will live,*

> *even though they die; 26 and whoever lives by believing in me will never die. Do you believe this?"* John 11:25-26

Jesus then quips back with strength in His words. He declares again here," I am." He says, "*I am* healing. I *am* faith. I *am* here. I *am* now. I *am* there for you. I *am* there for her. *I am* then. I *am* now. I *am* forever."

Then He asks her to believe only. "Believe only, Martha."

Personal is His call in our most desperate cries, in our most desperate situations.

> *27 "Yes, Lord," she replied, "I believe that you are the Messiah, the Son of God, who is to come into the world."* John 11:27

Look at dear Martha and her swift response to a seemingly impossible call to believe resurrection power for her dead brother, while the entire town is watching? While she stands there and hopes against hope that she could believe and it be true?

She declares Him to be the anointed One, the One waited for all those years, through all those desperate cries from all those generations of faith. Could it be true that He was actually there now for her? What was once a lofty concept becomes the moment of truth and belief.

> *28 "After she had said this, she went back and called her sister Mary aside. "The Teacher is here," she said, "and is asking for you." 29 When Mary heard this, she got up quickly and went to him. 30 Now Jesus had not yet entered the village, but was still at the place where Martha had met him. 31 When the Jews who had been with Mary in the*

> house, comforting her, noticed how quickly she got up and went out, they followed her, supposing she was going to the tomb to mourn there. 32 When Mary reached the place where Jesus was and saw him, she fell at his feet and said, "Lord, if you had been here, my brother would not have died." 33 When Jesus saw her weeping, and the Jews who had come along with her also weeping, he was deeply moved in spirit and troubled. 34 "Where have you laid him?" he asked. "Come and see, Lord," they replied. 35 Jesus wept. 36 Then the Jews said, "See how he loved him!" 37 But some of them said, "Could not he who opened the eyes of the blind man have kept this man from dying?"
> John 11:28-37

In that moment, all who were present had experienced darkness. And it was there, in the midst of that darkness that they experienced light and life, hope and expectancy.

Jesus Raises Lazarus from the Dead

> 38 "Jesus, once more deeply moved, came to the tomb. It was a cave with a stone laid across the entrance. 39 "Take away the stone," he said. "But, Lord," said Martha, the sister of the dead man, "by this time there is a bad odor, for he has been there four days." 40 Then Jesus said, "Did I not tell you that if you believe, you will see the glory of God?" 41 So they took away the stone. Then Jesus looked up and said, "Father, I thank you that you have heard me. 42 I knew that you always hear me, but I said this for

> *the benefit of the people standing here, that they may believe that you sent me." 43 When he had said this, Jesus called in a loud voice, "Lazarus, come out!" 44 The dead man came out, his hands and feet wrapped with strips of linen, and a cloth around his face. Jesus said to them, "Take off the grave clothes and let him go."* John 11:38-44

This is my story; perhaps it is yours, too. Jesus met me in the stench of a desperate and dying state. Although faith was distant and removed from my everyday life, He was there then and now. He kept His hand on me when my life did not show it. He met me when I thought all hope was lost. He resurrected my life from what it was destined to be to what He made it to be.

It is in knowing pain that I truly know His healing power. I can conclude that my pain has been a gift. The gift is an intimate and personal picture of how He shows Himself in contrast. I cannot know His weight of love until I have known and seen the weight of sin and despair. I would have had nothing to compare it to. His love, therefore, would not have been as precious to me, and I would not have found myself as desperate for it.

Just as Mary and Martha were desperate to hear the sound of God's voice, to watch Him bring light into the darkness that was before them, and just as I, too, have experienced that desperation and need, I can imagine that you know that pain full well. We do not pass through this life without loss, pain, heartbreak, fear, loneliness, and disappointment. It is how we invite God into that life that brings resonance of His kingdom work in us. This ultimately leads to great resurrection power of love and joy, peace, patience, kindness, goodness, meekness, gentleness, and self-control.

God is here. He is talking to you now.

THE WHISPERER

Listen intently, quietly, and with great expectation and the fullness of your faith, and you too will hear The Whisperer.

> *"The Lord thy God in the midst of thee is mighty; he will save, he will rejoice over thee with joy; he will rest in his love, he will joy over thee with singing."* Zephaniah 3:17

EPILOGUE

Because God Himself taught us to "hear and obey," our faith is increased with every step. There are so many parts of my life, my husband's life, and the lives of our children that had God-ordained outcomes that hinged on very specific obedience; obedience that was based not on easy decisions but confirmed through His love and plan for us. For example, my daughter Sarah would never have met her wonderful husband had she not known how to listen to God about leaving her volleyball experience in Austin. She now has three most beautiful children and her family is committed to hearing from God. My son Matthew, after a clear call from God; changed his plans and went to Baylor University. It was his confirmed destiny as he listened intently to God's still but resonating voice.

Likewise my daughter Rachel, after years of seeing a life of difficult decisions to follow Christ's call, followed Him straight out of her prolific athletic career to be alone at a university where she, too, has the confirmation of a life lived listening to God's voice. It is evident in her sweet family life that she and her husband know the sound of their Shepherd's voice.

Following God as He whispers His leading to us is a practice that can be difficult and usually includes laying one aspect of our comfort down for some discomfort. It can be frightening and cause doubt. On the other side of an obedient life, lies the confirmation that God is alive, real and concerned about the exact details of our lives. Peace follows. The confirmation rushes to our side as we, after hearing, can then see the plans God has for us. He wants a willing heart. He wants us in a place where we are willing to risk it all to follow Him. There is freedom there. Where He is leading, we cannot always be sure in the beginning; but it is always confirmed if we have eyes to see and ears to hear His glory in it all.

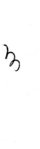

CPSIA information can be obtained at www.ICGtesting.com
Printed in the USA
LVOW04s1201170915

454201LV00002B/4/P